Teams
That Click

The Results-Driven Manager Series

The Results-Driven Manager series collects timely articles from *Harvard Management Update* and *Harvard Management Communication Letter* to help senior to middle managers sharpen their skills, increase their effectiveness, and gain a competitive edge. Presented in a concise, accessible format to save managers valuable time, these books offer authoritative insights and techniques for improving job performance and achieving immediate results.

Other books in the series:

Managing Yourself for the Career You Want

Presentations That Persuade and Motivate

Face-to-Face Communications for Clarity and Impact

Winning Negotiations That Preserve Relationships

A Timesaving Guide

THE RESULTS-DRIVEN MANAGER

Teams
That Click

• • •

Harvard Business School Press

Boston, Massachusetts

Library of Congress Cataloging-in-Publication Data

The results-driven manager: teams that click.
     p.   cm. — (The results-driven manager series)
  ISBN 1-59139-350-7
  1. Teams in the workplace. I. Harvard Business School Press. II. Series.
  HD66.R447 2004
  658.4′022—dc22

                                        2003021435

The paper used in this publication meets the requirements of the American National Standard for Permanence of Paper for Publications and Documents in Libraries and Archives Z39.48-1992.

Contents

Contents

Contents

Teams
That Click

Introduction

. . .

Think about your various experiences with teams. Do you recall a time when everything "clicked" on a team? When all the members felt a sense of belonging—a feeling of shared identity? When everyone eagerly embraced responsibility for achieving the group's collective goal and shared leadership of the project? When the longer its members worked together, the less oversight the group seemed to need? If so, you've had the good fortune to work on a highly effective team. When teams click, they generate extraordinary results that surpass the simple sum of the individual members' talents. Successful teams:

- Come up with more creative solutions to business challenges than individuals do

- Tap into the diverse skills of all their members

- Hone members' leadership abilities

1

- Catalyze fresh ideas for new products, better processes, and profitable strategies

- Carry out their mission with energy, efficiency, and dedication

- Engender feelings of satisfaction and pride in their work among members

- Channel conflict into productive directions

Teams that *fail* to click have their own distinctive characteristics as well. Members drag their feet when carrying out their responsibilities, can't make decisions, and get drawn into destructive interpersonal conflict. An atmosphere of boredom or passive resistance pervades the group. Ineffective teams may even fall victim to a kind of paralysis—some members stop attending meetings, while those who do show up have nothing to contribute.

If you've had the misfortune of participating in this kind of team, you know the costs: wasted time and money, mounting frustration, and projects neglected as the team spins its wheel uselessly.

Clearly, teams can make or break a manager's career—and even entire companies. Yet despite their potential to create important results for their members and organizations, few teams click successfully. Why? Leading teams—as well as participating in them—is difficult. Teamwork requires a deep understanding of group dynamics and the ways in which a team's unique "personality" emerges as the members accumulate a history of working together. Like couple relationships and great friendships, effective teams have a mysterious chemistry that's hard to tease apart and analyze. And in today's global business environment, cultural legacies can make teamwork even more challenging. Specifically, many Western businesspeople come from cultural traditions that emphasize individualism over collective achievement. Such people—whether they're team leaders or members—may find it difficult to think in terms of group-level accomplishment. In short, managing a team entails an entirely different set of skills than managing individuals.

Despite these difficulties, you *can* take steps to get the best possible results from the teams you're leading as well as those in which you're participating as a member. The articles in this volume help you by exploring four major themes:

- What makes a team click and how to boost collective productivity

- How to handle the inevitable conflicts that arise in any team

- How to deal with the special communication challenges that arise in cross-generational and virtual teams

- How to compensate and reward your team to further enhance performance

Let's examine these themes more closely.

Boosting Your Team's Productivity

As a manager, you work with teams every day—for example, to carry out a one-time product-development project, implement a long-term study on market segments, or improve your company's service-delivery processes. Some of the teams you work with may comprise your direct reports; others, peer managers over whom you have no formal authority. Teams may consist only of people from within your workplace, while some may have a "virtual" quality—they're made up of people who are working together from far-flung offices and entirely different time zones. Some teams you assemble yourself; others perhaps came together spontaneously to solve a pressing business problem. Finally, one team may comprise members who have similar backgrounds and work experiences, while another may contain a rich diversity of individuals from different generations, business functions, cultural backgrounds, and work styles.

In fact, if you've operated in the business world for a long time, you may find yourself working with teams more now than you did in the past. Why? Teams have played an increasingly central role in business as companies seek to "flatten" their reporting structures and drive needed changes in business processes and organizational culture. As leadership expert Daniel Goleman points out, "The team is the basic molecule of distributed leadership and the basic unit in which you can change norms throughout the organization." Effective teams also enable companies to unleash more creativity throughout their workforces than they would if they relied on "lone geniuses" to come up with profitable innovations. Often, teams come up with fresher ideas and solutions than individuals can.

Yet as Loren Gary affirms in "Managing a Team Versus Managing the Individuals on a Team," orchestrating team dynamics and individual dynamics requires two separate sets of skills. Unless you understand the difference, you may well stumble down the wrong path. To avoid that scenario, Gary recommends asking yourself four questions before you put a team together:

1. *Is a team the best organizational structure for your effort?* Rather than a team—which "pools its skills in a set of common work products" and shares leadership among the members—you might benefit more from a single-leader unit, or SLU. Single-leader units can produce faster in their early stages than teams can. They may thus prove a more appropriate structure if you're under time pressure.

2. *Have you established collective goals for the unit that members can personalize?* In successful teams, members "put their own slant on [the group's vision] . . . to create their own meaning out of the overarching vision."

3. *What signals are you sending to members about how the team should interact?* "The first few moments in the life of a team are really, really important," maintains Babson College professor Anne Donnellon. Members take one another's measure and look for a leader. Your job? To communicate the expectation that everyone will share leadership—by taking responsibility for carrying out the team's mission regardless of formal power positions.

4. *Does your performance management system reward interdependence and mutual accountability?* If not, it is unlikely that you'll turn a handful of disparate individuals into a smoothly functioning, effective team. Look for ways to evaluate and reward contributions to collective—not individual—goals.

If you've decided that a team versus an SLU structure would best suit your circumstances, you'll also need to know what distinguishes an effective team. Jim Billington's "The Three Essentials of an Effective Team" lays out these vital ingredients:

1. *Commitment.* Successful teams demonstrate shared dedication to the achievement of specific performance goals. "They invest a tremendous amount of time shaping a purpose that they then own." Participants "commit themselves to specific targets, and then hold one another accountable for their outcome." You know your team has real commit-

ment when members use "we" (for example, "We still have to design that market survey") and refer to one another in concrete terms ("Sue wants us to finish that product" versus "Management needs the product").

2. *Competence.* Too many companies mistakenly base membership in a team on formal titles or positions rather than skills. But members' core competencies strongly determine a team's effectiveness. In designing your team, seek three sets of skills: technical competence, problem-solving ability, *and* interpersonal talents.

3. *Common goals.* A team's goal differs from individual job objectives: It stems from a shared vision of why the team exists. Help your team establish its goal by "broadly framing what the company seeks from the team." Successful teams "invest tremendous time and effort in exploring, shaping, and agreeing on a purpose that belongs to them both collectively and individually." For example, a product-development team may have the overarching goal of increasing the division's innovation to meet the companywide goal of deriving half its revenues from new products.

Even teams with the above three characteristics can't succeed if their company as a whole doesn't support teamwork. In "Why Some Teams Succeed (and So Many

Don't)," the authors explain how managers can send a consistent message about the value of teamwork.

Here's a sampling of the guidelines: Strike the appropriate balance between yourself and your team—spelling out the team's objectives but leaving it up to the team members to decide how to achieve those goals. Provide training in teamwork skills, such as "listening, communicating with different kinds of people, and staying focused on the task." If at all possible, provide teams with opportunities to work together over a period of years. After all, nothing teaches teamwork better than actual experience. In addition, encourage members to design metrics for assessing their performance. And set up a steering committee to monitor the work of teams in your organization.

In "3-D Chess: Boosting Team Productivity Through Emotional Intelligence," Steve Barth focuses on the interpersonal skills required for successful teamwork. In particular, a team's members need a blend of self-management and relationship competencies to achieve "harmony and the ability to cooperate." But "a team's emotional intelligence is not simply the sum total of each *individual's* emotional intelligence skills." Rather, it's a trait that emerges at the group level as the members "manifest new strengths" together.

To bring out these strengths, a team needs three critical ingredients: *trust* (members share caring and concern for one another and view each other as honest and committed to the team's purpose), *group identity* (members "feel that they need the group, that the group needs them, and that their task is worthwhile"), and *group efficacy* (people feel confident that they can accomplish their task and do more by working together than carrying out their responsibilities separately).

Formal team leaders can help provide these ingredients by encouraging awareness and regulating emotions on three levels: *individual* (for example, start each meeting with a "check-in" that allows each member to describe how he or she is doing), *group* (acknowledge and discuss the team's moods, and communicate your sense of what's transpiring in the group), and *cross-boundary* (strengthen your team's relationships with other groups with which it must interact).

A team that cultivates its emotional intelligence vastly increases its capacity for innovation. Jim Biolos explores the phenomenon of team creativity in "Six Steps Toward Making a Team Innovative." To get *your* team's creative juices percolating, consider these guidelines: *Show confidence in your team* by modeling desired team-member behavior and setting appropriate goals. *Encourage free-flowing communication within the group*, ensuring that people feel comfortable expressing different viewpoints. *Give team members plenty of responsibility* so that they solicit new ideas from each other on how to get the project done. *Provide needed resources* and make sure people know they're available—that way, they won't have to waste time worrying about whether they'll get what they require to accomplish their tasks. *Give members challenging work* that they also find interesting. *Monitor pressure within the group* to strike the right balance between too much and too little (both of which stifle creativity).

Overcoming Team Conflicts

Mixing the right ingredients into your team's dynamics doesn't necessarily mean that conflict won't crop up once the group starts working together. In fact, every team experiences conflict. For example, people may disagree about the best way to handle a task or how to prioritize a project's responsibilities. Or one member might decide that another is being too stubborn, conservative, or critical. When conflict arises, emotions can run high. Before you know it, two team members are accusing each other of sabotaging the project, while another goes into a funk for weeks.

Yet even the most intense conflicts can actually prove beneficial—if you handle them skillfully. After all, without conflict, teams don't experience the differences of opinion that foster learning and creativity. Many groups become stagnant when members hesitate to disagree openly, and good ideas wither and die. Avoiding conflict at all costs can severely damage a team's effectiveness.

Loren Gary explores the dangers of conflict avoidance in "Bury Your Opinion, Shortchange Your Team." Often, he explains, team members don't openly disagree with one another for fear of derailing the group's work on a time-sensitive project. But then unexpressed differences fester, and the team misses out on the opportunity to exchange and challenge ideas. Distrust and fear set in, and relationships and decision making suffer.

To manage conflict more productively, develop team-based protocols for handling disagreements. For example, if a conflict arises between two people, discourage "triangulation"—the seeking of a third-party "rescuer" for resolution. Avoid actively recruiting supporters for your point of view and criticizing other team members when they're not present. View disagreements as a matter of organizational structure rather than personality clashes.

Jim Kling agrees with Gary on the importance of setting ground rules for managing conflict. In "Tension in Teams," he describes additional suggestions from various team-leadership experts. For example:

- Insist that conflicts be addressed right away.

- Stay with the tension and keep exploring creative options.

- Focus team members on the problem rather than on each other by listing issues on a whiteboard and arranging team members in a semicircle around it. You'll ally them against the conflict, instead of against each other.

In "Handling Conflict in Teams: A Roundup of Recent Research," the authors describe several personality types that can catalyze conflict within a team—and strategies for handling each type. For instance, to deal with a "show-off" (someone who needs to hear himself talk and constantly trumpet his own successes), offer a compliment as soon as he pauses for breath. Then switch the attention to someone else. With a "heckler" (an individual who interrupts every brainstorming session with criticism), challenge her to come up with something positive by asking, "What do you think *will* work in this proposal?" The authors offer strategies for handling additional "characters": "sotto voces" (people who make quiet sarcastic remarks), "mules" (people who resist all change), and "right but irrelevant ringers" (people with pet causes who simply won't be silenced).

Mattison Crowe pays special attention to silent malcontents in "Why the Members of Your Team Won't Speak Up, and What You Can Do About It." The author lays out six reasons team members don't express their opinions openly: 1) Members "give their proxy" to someone they perceive as an expert. 2) When a discussion seems to be going nowhere, people accept what seems to be a plausible solution. 3) Group members lack confidence in their ability to contribute. 4) The decision at hand strikes them as unimportant. 5) Individuals feel pressured to conform to the team's decision. 6) A dysfunctional decision-making climate pervades the team.

To solicit opposing viewpoints that stimulate dialogue and produce superior decisions, clarify the objectives the team is working toward. Inquire about the choices at hand; for example, "How would we respond to the concern that this decision might cause delays in the project?" And play devil's advocate—challenging assumptions and conclusions to generate alternative viewpoints for others to review.

Rebecca M. Saunders concludes this section with "Teams: Solving the Sophomore Slump." Saunders describes a troubling phenomenon that many teams encounter a year or so into a project: a "team midlife crisis." Members start showing up late or not at all. Those who attend meetings appear distracted. And "even if the team gets some things done, it isn't anywhere near as effective as during the first year."

Though this problem stems from a common human tendency to "run out of steam" after a long stretch of hard work, team leaders can still take steps to prevent it. For instance, they can spotlight the team's progress, teach team members new skills, and identify new team goals. Rotating team assignments and compensating members for extra work can also help replenish a group's energy.

Managing Communication Within Diverse and Virtual Teams

The articles in this section address two increasingly common types of teams: those comprising members from different generations, and virtual teams whose members operate from different offices and across different time zones. These team configurations raise unique communication challenges for managers.

In "Motivating Across Generations," David Stauffer explores the difficulties that arise in cross-generational teams. Four generations now participate in the U.S. workforce: "veterans" (age 59 and older), "boomers" (age 41 to 58), "Xers" (age 24 to 40), and "Nexters" (about 23 and younger). Members of each generation tend to share a unique perspective on work and preference for certain types of communication, and respond in predictable ways to specific motivators. To get the most from a cross-generational team, managers must customize the way they communicate with and motivate individuals from each generation.

For example, many veterans prefer face-to-face communication and live phone calls over voicemail, fax, and e-mail. They tend to respond to traditional forms of recognition, such as plaques, certificates, and photos with top executives. Numerous boomers want objectives stated in people-centered terms. They find team "pep talks" and widely noticed forms of recognition—such as articles in the company newsletter—highly motivating. Xers resist being told how to do their jobs. Time for fun, along with frequent and frank feedback, will likely motivate them. Nexters value opportunities for continuous learning and skill building. Coaching and informal communication (such as e-mails and brief hallway encounters) can serve as powerful motivators for this group.

The article "Virtual Teams: Paleolithic Insights About the Art of Cyber-Managing" shifts the focus to teams working interdependently across space, time, and organizational boundaries. With virtual teams, a sense of purpose and vision become particularly crucial to maintaining motivation and commitment among members who rarely or never meet face-to-face.

To establish a sense of group identity and avoid the misunderstandings that can proliferate in a virtual environment, leaders must constantly communicate with team members about expectations and norms for sharing information. They also need to encourage team members to "spell out what trust means to each of them. For example, trust may mean that if you send me an e-mail and ask for something immediately, I'll do everything possible to get back to you in three hours or let you know why I can't."

In "The Art of Managing Virtual Teams: Eight Key Lessons," Charles Wardell expands on these "cyber-management" ideas by offering additional guidelines. For instance, solidify your ability to manage an in-house team before you take on management of virtual teams. Once you've taken on a virtual team, check team e-mails daily for signs of conflict—then nip it in the bud by calling conflicted team members in person. Use phone conversations to probe for potential problems as well. If possible, have team members attend project kick-off meetings in person. Face-to-face contact can help clarify a sense of shared purpose and "light a fire in the belly" of every member.

Compensating and Rewarding Your Team

The way you compensate and reward your team plays as crucial a role in its performance as establishing a sense of shared identity, channeling conflict productively, and managing generational differences and distance. But team compensation and reward systems go far beyond merely salary raises or bonuses—and must be tailored to each team.

In "How to Compensate Teams," Loren Gary describes ways to customize your compensation system based on the type of team in question. For example, with *parallel teams* (those existing alongside the regular organizational structure), Gary recommends using an "add-on reward system, such as a gain-sharing plan, which quantifies cost reductions or other gains and, using a predetermined formula, distributes the gain among team members." With *project teams* (which bring together individuals from across functions to work on discrete projects over a lengthy time frame), consider linking compensation to completion of team tasks. And with *work teams* (self-contained, self-managed, and full-time interdependent units that produce a product or provide a service), use specially designed team incentives—such as merit pay in the form of salary increases or bonuses.

The article "How to Reward Project Teams" sheds additional light on strategies for project-team compensation. The authors argue that the form of compensation—whether it's an extra bonus, an incentive, or noncash recognition—for such teams matters less than the link between compensation and team goals and members' work reward values. To illustrate, if you offer cash payments, make them generous enough to capture team members' attention. Peg payments to measurable outcomes, and let members "divvy up the proceeds." With noncash awards—such as credit for purchasing company products, home-cleaning services, movie tickets, dinner out on the town—let team members know the dollar value of the various awards and allow them to choose how to "spend" it. A compensation that blends cash *and* noncash awards may prove the most effective.

Leading a team—regardless of its purpose, composition, and base of operation—presents special challenges for any manager. But by understanding the secrets to teams that click, knowing how to handle the inevitable conflicts that arise in any group effort, managing age differences and distance, and rewarding excellence shrewdly, you can boost the likelihood that *your* team will live up to its potential—and generate the business results that matter most to your company.

Boosting Your Team's Productivity

. . .

When teams click, their members feel a strong sense of commitment to a shared purpose. People embrace responsibility for fulfilling that purpose—regardless of formal authority hierarchies. Creativity and innovation run high, and members demonstrate energy and enthusiasm for the work.

The articles in this section explain what distinguishes successful teams and how to help *your* teams fulfill their remarkable potential. In addition to establishing "the three C's"—commitment, competence, and common goals—you'll need to cultivate your group's "emotional intelligence," that powerful blend of self-management and relationship skills that generates the most impressive results at the group level.

Your reward for blending the right team-performance ingredients in the right way? Fresh ideas, creative solutions to your most pressing business problems, and teams that perform with increasing excellence the longer they work together.

Managing a Team Versus Managing the Individuals on a Team

* * *

Loren Gary

The insight may steal upon you from any number of directions: Good coach that you are, you take one member of the team aside to tell her that she's doing a fine job. Three days later, word filters back to you that everyone else is annoyed because you singled her out for special attention. Or you move corporate heaven and earth to secure resources for the team, but none of its members seems even slightly grateful or particularly charged up.

Say hello to a critical piece of managerial learning: Managing a team is not the same thing as managing the individuals that make up a team.

What's the difference? Obviously this will vary based on factors like the task at hand and the make-up of the team. For example, are you using a team to plan the annual picnic or to devise the new product on which the company's future depends? Is the project a long-term or short-term one? Is the team composed of specialists, all of whom have longer tenure than you, or is it a group of your direct reports? To help you figure out your own situation and to assist you in maximizing your team's effectiveness, *Harvard Management Update* offers four questions to ask yourself, particularly in the early stages of putting a team together.

1: Is a team the best organizational structure for this effort?

Depending on what you're setting out to accomplish, you may not even need to get into the complexities of managing a team vs. managing individuals. Which is to say that in some instances, you may not want what Jon Katzenbach, a director at McKinsey & Co. and coauthor of *The Wisdom of Teams: Creating the High-Performance Organization,* calls a "real team." If, for instance, the necessity for speed in producing the work transcends other considerations, then you may be better off with a traditional single-leader unit, or SLU. Despite the almost ubiquitous use of the word "team" these days, most work groups don't fit that label at all, Katzenbach claims; rather, they are plain-old SLUs with a fancy '90s name. With a real team, says Katzenbach, "the leadership role shifts among the members of the group; an SLU, by comparison, always has the same leader. Moreover, a real team has to pool its skills in a set of common work products. In an SLU, the members don't do much collective work: they go into their offices and do work in their area of expertise, then bring it back to the group—and it's the leader who provides the integration.

"Although a real team can eventually produce at a higher level of quality and creativity than an SLU, it takes longer to get to the point where it is actually producing as a team. By contrast, with an SLU the leader knows what he or she needs from the outset, and can assign tasks out to the various unit members in ways that best match the members' skills. Consequently, the SLU can produce faster in the early stages."

While SLUs definitely have their place, their continued predominance in the workplace suggests that organizations may be missing out on the increased productivity that real teams offer over the long haul. To foster an environment in which an authentic team can come into being, you need to create the conditions where leadership can shift among all the members, and where team members are integrating the work themselves. And that, in turn, requires that the person with the hierarchical power—namely you—model the team-member behavior that you want to create.

2: Have I established collective goals for the unit that members can personalize?

"The onus is on management to articulate very clear collective objectives for the unit," says Susan G. Cohen, associate research professor at the Center for Effective Organizations at the University of Southern California's Graduate School of Business and one of the authors of *Designing Team-Based Organizations.* Such goals aren't simply a set of objectives for individuals that feed into the overall goal; there needs to be a mutual accountability to them, signaling that they must be shared. "The values and vision that lie behind the collective goals tie people into a greater whole," Cohen adds. "So it's important for the vision to be broad enough to enable individuals to put their own slant on it—to create their own meaning out of the overarching vision."

3: What signals am I sending to other members about how the team should interact?

"The first few moments in the life of a team are really, really important," observes Anne Donnellon, associate professor at Babson College and author of *Team Talk: The Power of Language in Teams.* "The team members are taking the measure of the one with the more formal authority in the group. The likeliest thing to occur in this situation is for the other members to sit back and wait for that person to tell them where to go and what to do. The best teams are the ones in which everybody takes responsibility—regardless of power position. The challenge for the team leader is to show that she is really interested in sharing power and responsibility; it's up to the team leader to create this context."

Managing "the process of the team's integration of its expertise" is crucial at this stage. For example, unless the manager resists the temptation to carry out the tasks himself, the other members will never believe that their talents are genuinely valued and will never understand that a higher level of accountability is being asked of them. "The big difference between managing individuals and managing a team is that team members are interdependent," Donnellon continues. "The more they work together, the less they need a manager." Overtly, as well as in subtle ways, the leader should encourage members to relate to each other, and not just to, or through, the leader.

It is only in this early stage, argues Katzenbach, when the members are still in the process of becoming a team, that the leader needs to be mindful of managing the individuals within the group. "Once the group becomes a team," he says, "it's able to manage individuals' needs and interests and feelings in different ways. The team leader shifts his modus operandi and is no longer called upon to serve as the single leader; he becomes something of a gap-filler within the workings of the team. This is one of the indices of a real team: Even the designated leader is doing real work, not just coordinating the work of others."

The leader should "propose and negotiate with team members, and take into consideration the limits and interests of the other members," Donnellon advises, instead of decreeing how things will be. Even with regard to a seemingly innocuous issue like setting regular meeting times, the inclusion of everyone on the team in this decision sends a powerful message about who matters and how the group is to function.

How the manager deals with someone who is expressing an opinion that is different from hers can be another watershed event in the early going. "People will be watching this interaction for clues about the leader's management style," Donnellon explains. "So it's very important to model good conflict [management]. Ask the person who's disagreeing to explain his position further, or to restate it so that you're sure you understand it. Acknowledge that the person may be right, and ask if there's any objective data to help resolve the difference of opinion. You want to model a style that says differences are okay, and that they should be engaged. This kind of approach signals to team members that their opinions count."

Donnellon characterizes this approach as being "authoritative without being autocratic." To the extent that hierarchical power has a place in teams at all, she explains, "it should reflect greater expertise or talent. But especially when dealing with a team of very talented members, the leader needs to use formal, hierarchical power very lightly. In fact, the more a leader can resist using hierarchical power, the more he can use informal means of influence, the better."

4: Does my performance management system actually reward interdependence and mutual accountability?

Even the most thoughtful attention to a team's formative stages will go only so far unless it's backed up by an appropriate performance-management regime—that is, a system for evaluating and rewarding contributions toward the collective goals. "But the problem with most traditional performance management systems," observes Cohen, "is that they're set up for the individual. They're based solely on a superior-subordinate [read: SLU] model. . . . Even the current rage in human resources circles, the 360° review, is still embedded in the logic of an individual evaluation: It doesn't deal with the performance feedback of the collective as a whole."

Establishing an appropriate performance management system often entails starting from the ground up, which means creating an evaluation instrument that measures collective performance first, and then individual contribution within that framework toward that goal. Cohen cautions, however, against becoming fixated just on short-term considerations, important as they may be. She explains, "Often a project's long-term implications aren't clear for several years, but there should be some attempt to take them into account nevertheless." For example, a software design team at Lotus Development Corp. tried to do this by including market share and long-term sales projections in the evaluation mix, along with the usual measures having to do with meeting the schedule, conforming to design specs, and debugging.

Just as the means of evaluation must change in order to accommodate an authentic team environment, so too must the reward procedures, says Cohen. A pay-for-skills system, or a competency-based pay system, "pays for the development of new competencies within the team; those new competencies, in turn, help improve the performance of the team. This approach has the added advantage of giving management some control over the definition of what competencies employees should be learning."

Constructing team bonuses for team success is doable but can be tricky. Cohen tells of an insurance company whose team bonus system actually had the effect of stifling cooperation among teams in different regions of the country. This is an area where a lot of work remains to be done. An individual's desire for recognition is a basic human need and must always be factored into any appraisal system. Cohen suggests, for example, that informal, everyday ways of acknowledging individual contribution often work best. But at your back, you still may hear those disputatious whisperings from the group: "Why her, if this is really supposed to be a team effort?" Won't somebody please figure out a way to still such mutterings with transparently fair, universally satisfying collective compensation?

For Further Reading

Designing Team-Based Organizations by Susan G. Cohen et al. (1995, Jossey-Bass, 419 pp.)

Team Talk: The Power of Language in Teams by Anne Donnellon (1996, HBS Press, 320 pp.)

The Wisdom of Teams: Creating the High-Performance Organization by Jon R. Katzenbach and Douglas K. Smith (1993, HBS Press, 304 pp.)

Reprint U9703A

The Three Essentials of an Effective Team

• • •

Jim Billington

Today the terms "team," "teamwork," and "managing the team" have come to stand for a wide swath of managerial practice that goes well beyond the actual use of self-managed work teams. An executive speaks of getting her team together for a meeting, or a security analyst writes of the "top management team" at such-and-such company, when neither of these assemblies of folks, whatever else their merits, would meet a sociologist's definition of how a true team interacts and performs. Indeed, "teamwork" has become the catch-all for almost every kind of management that seeks to differentiate itself from the bad old hierarchical, command-and-control-'em variety.

We also know that the use of teams in all their astonishing variety, including many that don't meet any traditional definition of the term, is on the increase. Organizations seek the greater creativity and productivity that teams offer. Individual employees want to be treated as team members, rather than as mere subordinates. Yet few teams live up to their potential—one of the reasons for the plethora of books on team building that cross our desk. Why do teams still so often fail after all the stories trumpeting their potential? (If you need a reminder, think of Team Xerox, Team Disney, and Kodak's Zebra Team.)

Given the current definitional muzziness coupled with hard-edged concern to improve the performance of these collections of people, we decided to look at just what distinguishes an effective team. A review of the recent literature suggests that there are three essentials: commitment, competence, and a common goal. Each is a little slippery, in that it may not look like what you'd expect, and you may have trouble detecting its presence—or absence—among the members of what you hope constitutes a team.

Commitment

The essence of a team is shared dedication to the achievement of specific performance goals, according to consultants Jon R. Katzenbach and Douglas K.

Smith, authors of *The Wisdom of Teams: Creating the High-Performance Organization.* The best teams invest a tremendous amount of time shaping a purpose that they then own. This front-end work requires all participants to commit themselves to specific targets, and then to hold one another accountable for their outcome. In other words, commitment comes from a shared sense of ownership of what the team hopes to accomplish.

Teams that issue from the minds of senior managers rarely elicit extraordinary performance from people. Katzenbach and Smith cite the example of a hastily implemented pilot-teams project launched by the Ritz Carlton hotel chain. The project had no specific performance goal other than the vague objective of "team building." By contrast, when the advertising division of the *Tallahassee Democrat* began to flounder, a project team of front-line workers sprang up to turn the division around. The newspaper's advertising business faced severe challenges from the likes of local television and cable, threats brought home by the fact that local papers around the country had begun to fold. The team's initial mandate was to eliminate errors in advertising, but after the group realized that the kinds of improvements it made could help ensure the continued existence of the paper, it tackled the problem of paperwork overload on sales reps and slow turnaround of advertising artwork. What began as a task force in effect became the un-official leadership of the entire newspaper. The difference was commitment—to one another, and to the clear goal of saving the newspaper.

How do you know when a team has real commitment, instead of just paying lip service to unrealistic goals? According to Anne Donnellon, author of *Team Talk: The Power of Language in Team Dynamics,* analyzing the language used by team members can uncover whether true commitment exists. For instance, when team members use the passive voice or third person pronouns to describe what they're doing—"That objective has yet to be realized," "It will get that new product out this year"—that's a warning sign. Is the team "it" or "we"? Another sign of trouble is the use of abstractions to describe people: "Management wants us to do this." When team members are genuinely committed, they reflect this fact by personalizing the language that they use. Donnellon's book gives specific guidelines for a "team talk audit" that can help a team understand itself better by monitoring the language it uses. For example, careful attention to how members use words can help smooth out misunderstandings caused by cultural differences. Being described as a "wild man" might be an accolade in Palo Alto but a slur in Zurich—just as working long hours may be taken as a sign of high commitment in Cleveland but could be perceived as an indicator of family troubles in Bordeaux.

Other experts agree that language is a major tip-off in distinguishing between a real team and one designed as "program of the month." In his provocatively titled book *No More Teams! Mastering the Dynamics of Creative Collaboration,* Michael Schrage derides the ubiquitous use of the term "buy in" to describe the work of building a team:

"When managers start talking about collaboration as 'buy in'. . . then collaboration comes to be seen as a political tool for alliance building rather than a genuine approach to creating value."

Commitment to a team tends to decrease as the number of people in the team increases. The experts concur on the point that teams of more than 20 people rarely reach exemplary performance. The ideal number of participants is ten or fewer.

> One of the myths about effective teams is that they are characterized by chumminess. Many look more like battlegrounds.

Commitment tends to increase with co-location—having team members working in the same geographic place, though our authors tend to disagree on how critical this component is. Schrage says that what he somewhat idiosyncratically terms "shared space" is all that is required—a blueprint or a clay model could be the only connecting point for collaborators on different continents. In *Teams and Technology: Fulfilling the Promise of the New Organization,* Don Mankin, Susan G. Cohen, and Tora K. Bikson describe ways in which information technology can enhance collaborative work without co-location. However, nearly all the examples of high-performance teams cited by the experts were co-located, at least at some point in their history. Videoconferencing and groupware do not substitute for the commitment that comes from human contact. Donnellon notes, too, that misunderstandings multiply when team members cannot speak face-to-face.

Another way teams build commitment is by allocating rewards based on the team's collective effort, not on individual performance. Schrage argues that nothing stifles team commitment more than The Boss claiming credit—and being rewarded—for the achievement of his team. And yet, so ingrained is the bias of American business in favor of individualism, that few companies have gone to the trouble of figuring out ways to evaluate and compensate people based on what their team has accomplished. On this front, Schrage offers practical suggestions for supplementing individual performance reviews with peer-evaluation and work-group reviews.

Competence

What can each member of the team actually do? Often overlooked in team architecture, the core competencies of its members are a critical determinant of how effective a team can be. Too many companies make the mistake of basing membership not on skills, but on formal titles or the position someone holds in the organization.

Katzenbach and Smith suggest that there are three sets of skills to seek in designing a team. The first is technical competence. Can the marketing person assigned really understand customers and help devise new ways to reach them? The second is problem-solving skill. Can she go beyond the neatly packaged duties she's used to performing to help make sense of a messy, complicated set of facts? The third is interpersonal skill. Can she communicate the insights from her technical background to members from other disciplines and contribute to a joint effort? Together these skills form the collective competence that will allow the team to succeed.

"Always being nice" is not on the list. According to Schrage, one of the myths about effective teams is that they are characterized by chumminess. Many effective teams look more like battlegrounds, it turns out. Highly competent designers clash with highly competent marketers. Teams with vastly competent members embrace conflict as the price of synergy and set good idea against good idea to arrive at the best idea. The Manhattan Project had many more physicists than team builders, and feuds raged throughout what was probably the largest collaborative project in history. But the result of great individual competence working toward a common goal was the realization of that goal. All the experts agree that, when managed properly, functional competence—

from individuals with great expertise, albeit in disparate disciplines—can aggregate to cross-functional success. Steven Covey summarizes this point by drawing the distinction between compromise and synergy. "Compromise," he observes, "is the proposition that $1 + 1 = 1.5$. Synergy is the proposition that $1 + 1 = 3$."

A Common Goal

At a recent conference, Covey also noted that one of the surest ways to reduce many teams to silence is to ask the question "Why do you exist?" When team members do not have a common vision of the purpose of the work they share, they cannot optimally work together. "Have you ever tried to put together a jigsaw puzzle," he asked, "with a number of people who all have a different picture of the finished puzzle in their mind? It's chaos." So, Covey says, "Begin with the end in mind."

A team's goal is different from the company's mission and from the sum of individual job objectives, Katzenbach and Smith observe. Direction from management may help a team get started by broadly framing what the company seeks from the team. The best teams then invest tremendous time and effort in exploring, shaping, and agreeing on a purpose that belongs to them both collectively and individually. This purpose must be measurable and attainable and should require roughly equivalent amounts of work from all team members.

For example, 3M has the company-wide objective of deriving half its revenues from products introduced in the last five years. Product-development teams at 3M's Occupational Health and Environmental Safety Division arose in the 1980s because traditional forms of organization weren't generating sufficient innovation to reach that goal. These teams were given autonomy and authority to establish their own goals, budgets, and objectives. But the overarching goal was never in doubt—to increase the division's product innovation to meet the companywide goal.

A goal that's been thrashed out, made clear, and widely agreed on can liberate the creativity of team members to experiment with new ways to reach the goal. Mankin and colleagues describe how to design teams that will encourage "tinkering" by the participants. As market conditions or customer needs change, so can the tactics of the team. The paradox is that the ends must be clearly understood before the means can be adapted. Designing a team to allow "for serendipity, spontaneity, and surprise" can only work when everyone fully understands and agrees on the objective. In the early days of Apple Computer, the collaboration between Jobs and Wozniak had from its start the goal of designing and building affordable personal computers. This consistency of purpose sustained the many iterations that it took to work out the specific details of a computer "for the rest of us."

Katzenbach and Smith offer another example of the power of a shared goal in the experience of the Burlington Northern Intermodal Team. With the deregulation of the railroad industry in the early 1980s, several managers at Burlington Northern saw an emerging opportunity for the "intermodal" shipment of freight—mixing truck and rail to optimize efficiency. When the Burlington Intermodal Team was formed, however, the team members had no blueprint for this new business concept. Train and truck operators distrusted one another, since they had competed directly in the old regulated environment. What united this seven-person team was the conviction that enormous efficiencies could arise from intermodal hauling. By the end of the decade, it had propelled Burlington Northern to leadership in a billion-dollar business. In the process, it helped reshape an industry. Its means changed repeatedly but not its goal. Said one team member: "The key word to this team was 'shared.' We shared everything. And the biggest thing that we shared was an objective and a strategy that we had put together jointly. That was our benchmark every day. Were we doing things in support of our plan?"

Commitment, competence, and a common goal aren't all that it takes to have an effective team. But they're the essentials with which to start.

For Further Reading

No More Teams! Mastering the Dynamics of Creative Collaboration by Michael Schrage (1995, Currency/Doubleday, 272 pp.)

Team Talk: The Power of Language in Team Dynamics by Anne Donnellon (1996, HBS Press, 320 pp.)

Teams and Technology: Fulfilling the Promise of the New Organization by Don Mankin, Susan G. Cohen, and Tora K. Bikson (1996, HBS Press, 320 pp.)

The Wisdom of Teams: Creating the High-Performance Organization by Jon R. Katzenbach and Douglas K. Smith (1993, HBS Press, 304 pp.)

Reprint U9701A

Why Some Teams Succeed (and So Many Don't)

The Key Is How They're Managed

• • •

Workplace teams have been studied to death in recent years, and the verdicts are in. They're a success—and a disaster. They lead to big productivity improvements—and they peter out ineffectively. People love 'em. People hate 'em.

In fact, says psychology professor J. Richard Hackman of Harvard University, researchers find that work teams cluster at opposite ends of the success continuum. Many function beautifully; many others fail miserably. Few are in in the middle.

The good news is that teams *have* been so well studied, and that people at so many companies have worked in teams for so many years. All this research and experience has produced new insights into what distinguishes the successes from the failures. What matters most, it turns out, is how teams are managed—and whether the organization they're part of provides them the support they need.

The Balancing Act

Managers responsible for team performance often fall into one of two traps. Some continue to act like traditional bosses, telling the team what to do and how to do it. Others think they're "empowering" the team by keeping hands off. Neither approach works. The manager's job, writes Hackman in a recent study of teamwork, is to "maintain an appropriate balance of authority" between himself and the team.

What does that mean in practice? On the one hand, managers have to spell out the team's objectives, unambiguously and unapologetically. That keeps teams from spinning their wheels over what they should be doing. "To authoritatively set a clear, engaging direction for a team," says Hackman, "is to empower, not depower, it." On the other hand, decision-making authority over the means to those ends should rest with the team itself. Team members can act as a team only if they have real responsibility—such as determining how to achieve their goals.

Practical experience has taught another lesson about teams' authority: the scope of their freedom of action can and should change over time. "What we encourage [managers] to do is start off very slowly and keep the boundaries pretty tight," says Tom Ruddy, manager of high-performance work systems and knowledge management at Xerox Worldwide Customer Services, which has depended on teams for many years. "As the team starts to grow and expand and take on responsibility, start moving those boundaries out." Even with successful teams, Ruddy says, a manager needs to remain involved. "They may have a lot of decision-making authority, but managers need to be looking at things a year out and showing where the teams will go next."

Learning Team Skills

Teams must be trained in teamwork: members often need help in skills such as listening, communicating with different kinds of people, and staying focused on the task. This is no news. But companies have learned—often the hard way—that the common approach of "train first and 'team' later" isn't effective.

A better alternative: periodic training over a period of time. "We used to bring [team members] into a room and take them through an intensive training," says

Successful Teams
What Makes Workplace Teams Work?

Researchers and Practitioners Identify Six Factors

1. A clear set of objectives, spelled out unambiguously by management
2. Metrics allowing team members to assess their performance—and showing the connection between the team's work and key business indicators
3. Ongoing training—not a one-shot deal—in communication, group leadership, and other team skills
4. Decision-making authority over how to reach their goals. But managers may need to start slowly and expand teams' scope of authority over time
5. Team-based rewards and evaluation, not individual incentives
6. An open culture, with easy access to team-specific information and to senior management

Ruddy. But team members didn't know what they needed to learn. Now Xerox spreads the training out: a session aimed at developing norms of behavior, for example, is followed by a few weeks on the job and then another session to revise the norms. "It's on-the-job training, rather than just 'inoculating' them all at once."

Experience also shows that nothing teaches teamwork like working on teams over a period of years. Members don't just have to learn new skills, they must also unlearn traditional roles. Linda Savadge, event coordinator at Educational Testing Service, has served on several teams. "It took a couple of years serving on different teams before the hierarchy within the team started to disappear," she says. At Xerox, members of one team realized they were so dependent on their manager that they had to take drastic action. "We told the manager he wasn't allowed to come to any meetings" until the team functioned better on its own, says Rick Crumrine, a customer-service engineer.

Goals and Metrics

Researchers have long known that any successful team is focused on performance. It has a well-defined set of goals and agreed-upon methods for achieving them. What's more, team members hold one another accountable for the performance of the whole group. These are the characteristics that distinguish a true team from a conventional department or work unit. "A team," wrote Jon R. Katzenbach and Douglas K. Smith in a now-classic *Harvard Business Review* article, "is a small number of people with complementary skills who are committed to a common purpose, set of performance goals, and approach for which they hold themselves mutually accountable" ("The Discipline of Teams," March–April 1993).

But goals and accountability require metrics allowing teams to assess their progress. One mark of a successful team is that members understand this fact, and begin to design their own measurements. Crumrine's team, for example, noticed some performance problems and created in-process measurements allowing them to evaluate their work day-to-day. "Instead of waiting for Xerox to send us information on how we'd done, we could check anytime during the month and see where we were at."

The latest insight on performance measurement: metrics need to be related to business goals, not just operational ones. Rather than pursuing a goal of better on-time delivery, say, teams need to focus on both the on-time rate and its business payoff—customer satisfaction, customer retention, and the like. "Teams need to understand the business ingredient of what they're doing and how they can affect that," says John Spencer, director of the Camera Technical Center at Eastman Kodak. Watching the bigger picture helps members balance multiple and sometimes conflicting objectives. It also helps them understand when it's time to declare victory—or defeat—and move on to another objective. "We have no problem saying, 'we're going to cancel this,'" says Spencer, since the teams at Kodak know the business reasons behind the decision and can "refocus around something that does make [business] sense."

Company Support

When teams first became popular, many companies established them—and promptly forgot about them.

Since then, researchers and practitioners have learned that successful teams require ongoing support from the whole company or business unit. That support may involve extensive changes. Orientation and training, for example, must be geared toward teamwork. Managers may need to be assigned to work on teams so they have first-hand experience with team-related issues. Joseph Reres, a partner with Potomac Consulting in Great Falls, Va., recommends that companies set up a "steering committee" to monitor the work of teams—and to make sure managers are helping rather than hindering teamwork.

Companies are just beginning to grapple with other forms of support, and not all have done so successfully. Two key areas:

Evaluation and compensation. "One of the hardest things for a company is to recognize that if they have installed teams, they need to reward based on teams," says Fritz Mehrtens, a leadership consultant in Irvine, Calif. "Companies say, well, we have an annual performance review and we give [individual] bonuses, promotions, and whatever based on that review. That tends to destroy the team—and it's a key part of the support structure that the company needs to change."

Information systems—and access. Teams can't function unless they get good information. IT departments, for example, may need to create systems that deliver team-specific data. And senior management must stand ready to give teams whatever other information they need. "That means the CEO shouldn't be upset if a team member walks into his or her office and says, 'I hear you said such-and-such and I need to know more about that,'" says Mehrtens. "The company needs to develop an open culture that allows team members to communicate wherever they want to."

On the face of it, says Harvard's Hackman, "the conditions that foster team effectiveness are simple and seemingly straightforward to put in place." Yet what's required for success can be a wrenching organizational change, threatening the turf and interests of powerful people inside the company. Indeed, setting up the conditions that make for successful teams is "more a revolutionary than an evolutionary undertaking."

That isn't an argument against team-based organization, which can have huge payoffs. But it is an argument for taking teams seriously, evaluating whether or not they can work, and doing what needs to be done to help them succeed. Left to their own devices, they won't make it.

For Further Reading

The Wisdom of Teams: Creating the High-Performance Organization by Jon R. Katzenbach and Douglas K. Smith (1994, HarperBusiness paperback)

Rewarding Teams: Lessons from the Trenches by Glenn Parker, Jerry McAdams, and David Zielinski (2000, Jossey-Bass Publishers)

The New Self-Directed Work Teams: Mastering the Challenge by Jack D. Orsburn and Linda Moran (2000, McGraw-Hill, 2nd edition)

Reprint U0001B

3-D Chess

Boosting Team Productivity Through Emotional Intelligence

* * *

Steve Barth

The team is the basic molecule of distributed leadership and the basic unit in which you can change norms throughout the organization," says psychologist Daniel Goleman, cochair of the Consortium for Research on Emotional Intelligence in Organizations at Rutgers University. With so much riding on these interactions, companies cannot afford to view the role of emotions in group performance as a messy nuisance that must be "dealt with" only as a last resort.

In his popularizing books *Emotional Intelligence* (Bantam, 1995) and *Primal Leadership* (HBS Press, 2002), Goleman portrays emotions as an evolved signal system and emotional intelligence (EI) as the process of learning to be aware of and to regulate one's emotions. EI accounts for as much as 70% of individual performance, he maintains, whereas cognitive ability and technical learning account for only 30%.

Most of the emotional intelligence research conducted so far addresses one-on-one relationships. The field's cutting edge involves the application of EI principles to catalyze the productivity of teams. Not every team requires high emotional intelligence, but for those that do, there's no substitute for EI. "It's not just a warm-and-fuzzy," says Sandra Yingling, Ph.D., a Walnut Creek, Calif.–based senior consultant at Hay Group's organizational effectiveness and leadership development practice. "It unlocks productivity and creativity in a way that nothing else does." Specifically, an effective team must know how to play the EI equivalent of three-dimensional chess: "It must be mindful of the emotions of its members, its own group emotions or moods, and the emotions of other groups and individuals outside its boundaries," write Vanessa Urch Druskat and Steven B. Wolff in "Building the Emotional Intelligence of Groups" (*Harvard Business Review*, March 2001).

From Individual to Group Performance

In some consultants' use of the term, emotional intelligence amounts to little more than the ability to be tactful. But for University of New Hampshire psychology professor John D. Mayer, one of the EI pioneers, the term has a very precise meaning. "It's the ability to reason with and about the emotions, and the capacity of emotions to reach into the cognitive system to help us reason better," he says. EI is not innate—it's an ability that can be learned and improved. Financial advisors at American Express who took a 12-hour training course were able to increase emotional competencies by 15% while boosting their business performance by 18%, notes Kate Cannon, former director of leadership development, who administered the training. Regions whose sales managers received EI training had sales results that were 11% greater than regions that didn't. The bottom-line impact was estimated at $200 million in additional annual sales.

Cannon's results speak to the importance of developing emotionally intelligent *individuals.* But a collection of emotionally intelligent individuals does not an emotionally intelligent team make. "Everybody assumes you will be fine if you have smart, motivated people in the room," says Druskat, assistant professor of organizational behavior at Case Western Reserve University. "But some of the worst teams have the best people on them."

Research has demonstrated "the superiority of group decision making over that of even the brightest individual in the group," write Goleman, Richard Boyatzis, and Annie McKee in *Primal Leadership.* The one exception, however, is when the group lacks harmony or the ability to cooperate. In such instances, "even groups comprising brilliant individuals will make bad decisions."

Lay the Foundation by Establishing Norms

A team's emotional intelligence is not simply "the sum total of each individual's emotional intelligence skills," says Goleman. "What happens is that there is an emergent property at the team level where, as a group, people together manifest new strengths." To bring these strengths out in your group, you need three critical ingredients, says Druskat:

Trust. Team members need to have reciprocal care and concern for each other and to have faith in each other's honesty and commitment.

A group identity. When team members make the group's goals their own, they feel that they need the group, that the group needs them, and that their task is worthwhile.

Group efficacy. Team members need to be confident not only that they can accomplish the task but also that they can accomplish more working together than separately.

The order is significant here. Each ingredient builds on the one before, which makes trust paramount. But you can't assume that people will be open and honest with each other from the start. A trusting environment can only be constructed through the slow, incremental work of noticing other group members' emotional reactions and making intelligent decisions that take their feelings into consideration. Members need a chance to get to know one another and work through any latent history—a consequence of their having formed opinions of one another based on limited prior contact. They may also be skeptical of the reasons for forming the team,

The thirst for direction is especially evident in teams of high performers.

suspicious of the politics, or resentful of the extra work involved. Countering such attitudes is sometimes more a matter of small actions that have far-reaching consequences than of sonorous pronouncements about values. Group EI, write Druskat and Wolff, is often not as much about an in-depth discussion of ideas as it is about "asking a quiet member for his thoughts." It is not so much about a "lack of tension, and all members liking each other" as it is about "acknowledging when harmony is false, tension is unexpressed, and treating others with respect."

"A lot of the emotional challenges that teams face are values conflicts, where people are judging each other or assume others should perform or say things differently than they do," says Cannon. Consider the mix of cultural values on an international team—even basic concepts such as honesty can have completely different meanings. Sometimes differing functional perspectives create the challenge. With a cross-functional product development team, for example, representatives of different units may give different weights to performance, safety, and cost. At other times the source of the challenge lies in members' attitudes about expressing emotion. Cannon recalls an American Express team in which low self-esteem prevented members from voicing doubts or asking for help. "If people can't bring these things to the team, they are probably withholding bad news, such as that a project isn't going as well as it needs to, and that contributes to delays and missed goals," she says.

Don't underestimate the power of unstated norms to govern a group's behavior. Two stories from *Primal Leadership: Realizing the Power of Emotional Intelligence* serve as cases in point:

- A new leader blew in to the sleepy division of an insurance company without grasping its emotional reality—the tight cohesion of its members. Everyone turned against her, and the division's performance tanked.

- "Consensus usually results in highly committed and motivated team members," write Goleman, Boyatzis, and McKee, but in one particular division of a health care company, the leader was using the consensual approach "as a way to stall and even hijack decisions—especially decisions that would move things in a new direction." As a result, the division was overstaffed and hemorrhaging cash, yet still providing inferior service. The lesson here: sometimes the unstated norms, though rooted in laudable goals, can become dysfunctional.

The Leader's Role

Group norms get introduced "by formal team leaders, by informal team leaders, by courageous followers, through training, or from the larger organizational culture," write Druskat and Wolff. The ways that informal leaders or followers can enhance the group's emotional intelligence are often subtle, as when an individual points out how the team is "ignoring an important perspective or feeling."

In many instances, however, the work of surfacing deeply embedded norms or establishing new norms falls to the formal leader. A recent Hay Group study highlights ways the leader can help create "the conditions that encourage team members to deepen their commitment": Encourage members to speak out whenever they disagree with an issue related to team goals, and also to speak for those who aren't present. Don't let one person's absence allow other members to drive through a proposal the absent person would have objected to. But once the group has decided upon a course of action, insist that members support it, regardless of whether they agree with it.

Using Emotional Intelligence Tests to Improve Team Performance

"Typically, individuals' assessments of their own EI are not highly correlated with their actual emotional intelligence," says John D. Mayer, professor of psychology at the University of New Hampshire, which is why testing an individual's ability or performance can be an important part of developing your team's capabilities. But when you're looking for a test to use, scrutinize the options carefully. As you'll see from the descriptions of the three tests listed below, each one measures something different.

1. The ECI-360, developed by psychologist Daniel Goleman and Hay Group, defines EI as a set of abilities and personality traits. It looks at four broad domains—self-awareness, self-management, social awareness, and relationship management—that are subdivided into 18 different competencies. Among them: self-confidence, adaptability, emotional self-control, and the ability to inspire and to manage conflict.

2. The EQ-i, developed by Israeli psychologist Reuven Bar-On, is perhaps the most extensively normed EI test to date. It, too, defines EI as a mixture of abilities and personality traits, but the combination is different from that in the ECI-360. For example, the EQ-i seeks to measure a

respondent's stress tolerance, problem-solving ability, and level of optimism and happiness.

3. The soon-to-be-released MSCEIT views EI purely as "a set of mental abilities," write Mayer and codevelopers Peter Salovey and David Caruso in "Emotional Intelligence and Emotional Leadership" (an article in *Multiple Intelligences and Leadership*). Its four categories test for the ability to (1) "differentiate between real and phony emotional expressions"; (2) use emotions to facilitate decision making and problem solving; (3) understand complex relationships among emotions; and (4) "solve emotion-laden problems without necessarily suppressing negative emotions."

How might you use one of these tests? Mayer recounts the story of a supervisor who grew concerned that something was amiss with his team, which worked independently of the main office, even though everyone said things were going great. After having all the members take the MSCEIT, the supervisor discovered that one person had a very low EI score. It turned out that this employee was underperforming, but because he was politically connected to another supervisor in the firm, his fellow team members felt that they couldn't criticize him. They were essentially covering for the bad apple on the team, and the EI assessment helped the supervisor diagnose the problem.

The formal leader's role in building group identity and efficacy is particularly important. When the leader fails to provide clarity about the team's purpose, "a leadership vacuum is created, one that all members rush to fill with their own individual priorities and goals," notes the Hay study. This thirst for goals and direction is especially evident among high performers. On outstanding top teams, "the leader gave far clearer direction than on average or poor-performing teams."

And how should you provide that clarity? As with most things, style matters. Of the six leadership styles that Goleman identifies in "Leadership That Gets Results" (*Harvard Business Review*, March–April 2000), the Hay study observes that outstanding teams prefer either an *authoritative* style, in which the leader is the one who sets the vision, or a *democratic* style, in which team members are allowed "to participate in fleshing out the vision articulated" by the leader. Interestingly, the *pacesetting* style, exemplified by the leader who is always modeling the desired behavior but who often feels "compelled to rescue team members who are struggling," does not get high marks—it makes members feel disempowered.

Working in Three Dimensions

Think of the task of building an emotionally intelligent team as establishing norms that create awareness of emotions and regulate those emotions once they're identified. This work should take place on three levels:

- **On the individual level,** actions that create awareness of emotions include having a check-in time at the start of each meeting to see how everyone is doing and questioning decisions that seem to be made too quickly. To help regulate individuals' emotions, set ground rules for what constitutes errant behavior and come up with playful means of pointing out such behavior. "Validate members' contributions," write Druskat and Wolff, and protect members from attack.

- **At the group level,** acknowledge and discuss the team's moods; communicate your sense of what is transpiring in the group. Find shorthand methods of expressing the group's emotions and fun ways of relieving stress. To help create an affirmative environment, remind members of the importance of the team's purpose and of how they have successfully solved similar problems in the past. Focus on the things you can control.

- **Interactions on the cross-boundary level** can be the most difficult. A team that is keenly aware of its own emotional dynamics can be oblivious to the needs of key outside groups, says Druskat.

Set aside meeting time for ascertaining the needs of groups that can help your team accomplish its goals. Strengthen these external relationships by creating opportunities for interaction—for example, invite an outside group to one of your team meetings if that group has a stake in what you're doing. Build organizational understanding by discussing the culture and politics of your company.

Of course, EI is more important for some teams than for others. Teams with high customer contact require highly developed emotional skills—not so for finance or IT teams, which focus on technical issues. Preliminary findings from one study of finance professionals suggest that those with higher performance evaluations tend to have lower EI scores, says Mayer. For such teams, ensuring that at least one member has a high EI may be sufficient.

"There's a saying, 'I've been rich and I've been poor—and let me tell you, rich is better,'" concludes Mayer. "Emotional intelligence is like that. Developing high emotional intelligence for its own sake is nice, but most companies aren't in a position to do that." So implement the principles of emotional intelligence strategically, focusing on those teams for which EI can have the greatest impact on performance.

For Further Reading

Primal Leadership: Realizing the Power of Emotional Intelligence by Daniel Goleman, Richard Boyatzis, and Annie McKee (2002, HBS Press)

Multiple Intelligences and Leadership edited by Ronald E. Riggio, Susan E. Murphy, and Francis J. Pirozzolo (2002, Lawrence Erlbaum Associates)

Top Teams: Why Some Work and Some Do Not (2001, Hay Group)

Reprint U0112B

Six Steps Toward Making a Team Innovative

. . .

Jim Biolos

Too often we think of creativity as the province of individuals—the lone genius out there hatching the bright idea. But as more work gets done in teams, two new realities of corporate creativity have become apparent. First, teams can indeed come up with novel solutions to business problems, often fresher ideas than any single person in the organization can generate. Second, teams do not perform this magic automatically—the process must be managed. But how?

To find out, a research effort headed by Harvard Business School Professor Teresa Amabile has begun exploring the distinctive dynamics of creativity and innovation in work-group or team environments. To do this, Amabile developed a survey, called KEYS: Assessing the Climate for Creativity, for measuring these conditions. In studies that laid the groundwork for the current project, Amabile and her team interviewed executives, team leaders, and team members in several different organizations. The interview asked participants to identify the successful creative projects they had been involved with, and to talk about how they carried these projects beyond the "light bulb goes on" stage. "All innovation begins with creative ideas," Amabile explains. "Successful implementation of new programs, new product introductions, or new services depends on a person or team having a good idea, and then developing that idea beyond its initial, ill-formed state."

Amabile and her colleagues identified six conditions evident in successfully creative project teams. Each is something that a team manager can encourage, if not always put in place single-handedly. Understood as action steps, some may seem reminiscent of old, conventional, hierarchical wisdom, but in fact each has subtleties that you can easily miss—at your peril.

1: Show Confidence in the Team

Inspirational speeches, if that's all you're providing, won't suffice. The team will look to you to demonstrate your confidence in their efforts both by your modeling good team-member behavior (valuing individual contributions, for instance) and by more leaderly actions (setting appropriate overall goals, making sure that the group's needs are met). If the team leader doesn't exhibit enough confidence, the team will usually sense this and respond by throttling back on its own enthusiasm for the project. Such disengagement, Amabile found, generally means less curiosity and creativity, and less of the impassioned dialogue that leads to breakthroughs.

2: Make Sure That the Members of the Group Are Communicating Freely with One Another

And make sure there are enough differences in their viewpoints that they have something interesting to say to each other. The ideal is a team with a diverse set of backgrounds with differing skills who nonetheless trust each other enough to challenge one another's work as part of a general openness to new ideas.

As a manager, your responsibility begins with identifying the right mix of members for the project team. Diversity does not necessarily mean along ethnic or gender lines, although that often helps. It can mean bringing marketing, finance, and information-technology people together for a full airing of their different views of a particular subject. You've heard (probably many times) the old saying that "The best ideas come from the strangest places." Creative teams are no exception, with the intersection between colliding views and ideas representing what may seem at times—including to the participants—like a pretty strange, occasionally contentious place. Pick your team members carefully; get the right mix of functional skills, conceptual thinkers, and people unafraid to question others. Amabile found that a homogeneous group whose members are prone only to agree with one another will typically not promote high levels of creativity.

3: Make Sure to Give the Team Members Enough Responsibility

If you take control of too much—for example, deciding exactly what work is to be done, when and how—you will inhibit your team's ability to think and act creatively. Each group member should feel unfettered to carry out his or her piece of the project. On the other hand, giving team members more responsibility does not mean dumping piles of work on them without providing direction. What you want to achieve is a balance, the chief sign of which will be team members soliciting new ideas from each other on how to get the project done.

4: Provide the Appropriate Resources to the Team

Ensure that your team is comfortable, in the sense that people can spend their time thinking creatively about using those resources instead of worrying about whether they'll be made available. Too often project leaders are either visibly unsure about their ability to marshal what's necessary—people, money, equipment, information, or access—or they fail to tell team members that the resources are available. If there are resource constraints, have the team help you evaluate them. You'll be better able to determine the resources the team simply has to have, and better able to make the case to senior management for getting them.

5: Make Sure That Each Team Member Has Challenging Work

It is not enough for people just to be assigned to the project—they need to be doing work toward goals that they find interesting. Amabile found that when people feel challenged by their job—but not unreasonably challenged—they tend to be much more creative than when tasks are either too simple or impossibly difficult. So again, the manager has to achieve a certain balance. Ways to introduce more challenge into a team's work include having members learn from one another, take on new responsibilities, and avail themselves of opportunities for sharing their expertise in new ways with new groups of people. Push all members of the team to explore the outer reaches of his or her capabilities; ask them to think about their function in new ways. Then watch carefully for overload.

6: Monitor the Pressure

According to Amabile's findings, pressure can inhibit creativity if it is too strong or too weak. When team members are under extreme time pressure or have been set unrealistic productivity targets, their creativity will be stifled. You will begin to hear complaints about having too much work and too little time to complete it. But at the other extreme, when a team member does not have enough work or deadlines to work against, you may not get her best ideas, highest levels of motivation, or even her attention. As a rule, team leaders too often use pressure to get the job done. Wise managers pick their spots for applying pressure, regulate it constantly, and ease up when necessary. But the pressure should never seem arbitrary—it should come across as an indicator of the urgent need for, and the ultimate value of, the work being tackled.

These six action steps may seem obvious, but getting them right may take a long time. Amabile's research suggests that you don't engineer a creative environment overnight—it can take months to develop. Successful managers incorporate these conditions gradually, subtly, and consistently over time.

Set goals for establishing the team's work environment and for assessing that environment. And set time frames for yourself. By what month do you want your team to be showing freer-flowing communications? How do you intend to foster that? How will you know when the team has arrived—by what measures?

Remember: You're creating a new culture. This takes time and effort, but done right, you'll take pride in ideas that your team will produce.

For Further Reading

The Wisdom of Teams by Jon Katzenbach and Douglas Smith (1993, HBS Press, 304 pp.)

KEYS: Assessing the Climate for Creativity by Teresa M. Amabile (1995, available through the Center for Creative Leadership)

Reprint U9608C

Overcoming
Team Conflicts

• • •

No team can avoid conflict—nor should it try to. Disagreements and tension can provide the energy that fuels new, unexpected ideas and fresh alternatives—*if* you channel conflict in productive directions.

The selections in this part of the book offer guidelines for managing tension within teams, encouraging members to disagree openly and constructively, and establishing ground rules for the productive resolution of disagreements. You'll also discover strategies for preventing "team midlife crisis"—a slump in energy that strikes many teams a year or so after they begin working together.

Bury Your Opinion, Shortchange Your Team

• • •

Loren Gary

Last year, David MacNair, a senior vice president for Campbell Soup, detected a problem in his Camden, N.J.-based unit's leadership team. "The team had developed an acute case of silo behavior. People didn't seem to feel the need to interact," he says. "We were functioning adequately as a group of individuals with busy jobs. But we weren't really functioning as a team."

The problem, MacNair explains, was that "team members were more comfortable talking to me about issues than to one another. They got along with one another all right, but their interactions were purely functional; they weren't engaging one another as members of a senior team with joint responsibilities for such issues as resourcing, human development, budgeting, and communications."

> The management of conflict is not simply an interpersonal matter—it must become an organizational competency.

Management literature tends to focus on the kind of conflict characterized by interpersonal hostility. But the pattern of submerged or silenced differences of opinion that MacNair describes here is just as pernicious—and perhaps even more widespread. And when leaders are unaware of their own differences of opinion and unable to address them, everyone else in the unit pays the price. The sources and handling of conflict in leadership teams, therefore, deserves special attention.

Three books shed light on this subject. All acknowledge that it's not only impossible to eliminate conflict entirely but that you wouldn't want to—without conflict, you wouldn't have the differences of opinion that foster learning and creativity.

Even so, it is important to keep unacknowledged differences among team members from festering into destructive conflict and to manage conflict once it has surfaced. After a conflict has been acknowledged, the more you can depersonalize it and treat it as an organizational issue—for example, by setting up protocols for how employees who are at odds should treat one another—the better off you'll be. But to break the code of silence that helps keep differences of opinion underground, you have to be willing to take a personal risk.

The Silent Spiral

"Conflict-management strategies take for granted that you have a difference of opinion with someone and that you know what it is," says Harvard Business School professor Leslie A. Perlow. "In many instances, however, people aren't even aware that there's a difference because they've been silencing others' opinions and also their own."

Silencing takes many forms, observes Perlow in her book *When You Say Yes but Mean No: How Silencing Conflict Wrecks Relationships and Companies . . . and What You Can Do About It.* Sometimes a supervisor suppresses a subordinate's differing opinion by conveying the idea that the advice is unwelcome. But silencing is also something we do to ourselves. We do it when we're dealing with our bosses, our peers, even our subordinates. And we do it with the best of intentions, Perlow says. Sometimes "people silence themselves because they truly believe that's what's best for themselves, their relationships, and the company." For example, a person might not express her disagreement for fear of derailing the team's work on a time-sensitive project.

When we act as if there is no difference of opinion, it does not disappear, notes Perlow. "Instead, it causes us to become self-protective in our relationship, and the climate in the relationship quickly disintegrates to one characterized by distrust and fear, making us all the more likely to silence in the future."

The resulting organizational damage can include broken relationships, diminished creativity, impaired learning, and poor decision making. In 1997, managers at Samsung didn't question a $13 billion investment that would take the company into the automobile industry because the idea's champion, Samsung Chairman and CEO Kun-Hee Lee, was a forceful personality and a car buff. When Samsung Motors folded only a year into production, Lee wondered why no one had expressed reservations.

To prevent such mistakes, companies must "replace vicious silent spirals with virtuous spirals of speaking up," writes Perlow. You must be willing to take the risk of expressing your differences of opinion openly and honestly, but also strategically—in groups in which you have some standing and influence, and in situations in which airing the difference is important to the work of the group or the relationships involved. The task is one of seeking mutual understanding, Perlow writes. Although leaders play a crucial role in modeling this behavior and rewarding it in others, "everyone needs to take responsibility for speaking and listening in a way that not only ensures clear communication but also makes it easier for others to speak up."

Seeing Others' Perspectives

The strategies for achieving mutual understanding don't just help prevent the silent spiral, they can also help bring to the surface the hidden agendas that abound in leadership teams and help managers deal with them. "You need to create a space—public or private—to talk about the unspoken differences," says Deborah M. Kolb, a professor at the Simmons School of Management in Boston and coauthor of *Everyday Negotiation: Navigating the Hidden Agendas in Bargaining*. Start by demonstrating your reflexivity—your willingness to see how you may have contributed to the conflict. From there, "try to have an appreciative conversation in which you legitimate other people's perspectives and make it possible for them to talk about how they got to their position on an issue."

This goes beyond notions in the negotiation literature about intellectually understanding another person's perspective, Kolb emphasizes. "You can't create a connec-

tion across difference unless you understand the concrete situation in which the other person is acting. You
can't know that situation well beforehand—just by trying to imagine what it must be like. You have to create a
space in which the other person can talk freely. That
said, a strategy that can help put you in a connected
frame of mind is to think of good reasons that the other
person would use to justify his own position or behavior.
Don't just think of one; try to come up with five."

Organizational Support

Leadership teams often need help developing the skills
of active listening and reflexivity that make productive
conversations about conflict possible. But the preven-
tion of the silent spiral and the management of conflict
are not simply interpersonal matters—they must become
organizational competencies, argues Howard M. Guttman in *When Goliaths Clash: Managing Executive Conflict to
Build a More Dynamic Organization*. The more thorough
the discussion of a company's strategic and key operational goals, the less the likelihood that significant differences of opinion will go unexpressed. The same goes
for individual accountabilities. "Ask team members to
list the activities that they carry out and the results that
they are responsible for," writes Guttman, "to describe
how they believe their job is perceived by other players,

and to identify the gaps that exist between themselves and the other team members."

It also helps to develop team-based protocols for handling conflict. For example, when the conflict is just between two people, don't triangulate by looking to a third-party rescuer for resolution. Don't actively recruit supporters for your point of view. Don't criticize other team members when they're not present.

Above all, try not to personalize issues. Organizational structure, rather than personal dislike, often lies behind differences being submerged. "I realized that by allowing the team members to deal primarily with me," Campbell Soup's MacNair says, "I was inadvertently enabling them to avoid conflict among themselves."

For Further Reading

When Goliaths Clash: Managing Executive Conflict to Build a More Dynamic Organization by Howard M. Guttman (2003, AMACOM)

Everyday Negotiation: Navigating the Hidden Agendas in Bargaining by Deborah M. Kolb and Judith Williams (2003, Jossey-Bass)

When You Say Yes but Mean No: How Silencing Conflict Wrecks Relationships and Companies . . . and What You Can Do About It by Leslie A. Perlow (2003, Crown Business)

Reprint U0305B

Tension in Teams

When Is It Destructive, When Is It Creative?

• • •

Jim Kling

The product development team imploded the last time you launched a new product. Dwayne in engineering and Laura in marketing argued endlessly over the timing of the product introduction. The VP of finance jumped in when Dwayne insisted on increasing the development budget to meet Laura's deadline. And then Laura accused him of sabotaging the whole project. As team leader, you eventually forced a compromise, but Dwayne was convinced that his competence as an engineer had been challenged, and he went into a funk for months.

Now, it's time to start assembling the team for a new project. You can't ostracize Dwayne—he's the best engineer you have. So how do you keep the inevitable conflicts from tearing your team apart?

You're probably asking yourself how you can avoid conflict altogether. But it's the wrong question. Conflict is inevitable, and it can be the single best fuel for the creative fire. Without it, teams become stagnant and good ideas wither and die. "As William Wrigley, Jr. used to say, 'If two people in business always agree, one of them is unnecessary,'" says Paul Hennessey, executive VP of marketing, research, and development at BayGroup International, a consulting and training organization in Larkspur, Calif.

The right question to ask yourself is: How can I manage the conflict to get the best solutions out of the team?

First and foremost, it will probably take some re-education. "People have grown up with the idea that conflict is bad and uncomfortable, so you should by all means avoid it," says Morris R. Shechtman, chairman of the Shechtman Group (Kalispell, Mont.). "That starts with the top decision makers, who are consummate conflict-avoiders."

Although conflict avoidance can seem like the best solution in the heat of the moment, it often causes a snowball effect. For example, when Laura insisted that the product should be ready to ship in time for the trade show in April, Dwayne knew right away that it would be a tight squeeze to make that deadline. But he chose not to speak up, because it might have called into question his ability to deliver on time. So Dwayne went back to his office and stewed about it, and when Laura mentioned the trade show again at a meeting the following week, he released his pent-up frustration and told her the trade show didn't matter, this was a difficult engineering problem, and just who was she anyway to be setting deadlines for the engineering team? Needless to say, the rest of the meeting wasn't very productive.

How could you, as team leader, avoid this scenario and turn the conflict into something positive? Experts offer some advice.

First, Set a Few Ground Rules

One of the keys to managing conflict in teams is to set up ground rules in advance. "It's not my experience that chaos inherently results in brilliance, although sometimes that is the case," says Stever Robbins, president of VentureCoach.com (Cambridge, Mass.). Instead, it's a good idea to set guidelines to help work through disagreements.

The most important rule: conflict should be handled openly. "Give them two options: confront the conflict and handle it, or let it go," says Howard Guttman, principal of Guttman Development Strategies, Inc. (Ledgewood, N.J.). "Those are the only two acceptable options. Lobbying around the water cooler and sending scud missiles by e-mail should be verboten."

In other words, insist that conflicts get addressed right away. "As soon as I notice something, I get it on the table and address it directly," says Shechtman. "You want a feedback-rich environment where it is each team member's responsibility to bring up what bothers them," he says.

And when the feedback hits the fan, don't always take the easiest road to defusing conflict. "Stay with the tension," says Hennessey. "In our work the best teams and their leaders are able to 'hang in there' with the tension and keep exploring creative options. It's much more likely that innovative solutions will emerge."

To keep things from getting too personal, you can physically arrange team members so that they are focused on the problem and not on each other. "Put the items on a whiteboard and place team members in a semicircle around it so that they are allied against the conflict," suggests Robbins.

Every team is unique, and individual personalities will dictate some of the conflict-management rules. Jeff Weiss, a partner at Cambridge, Mass.–based Vantage Partners LLC, suggests that teams brainstorm in the beginning to come up with worst-case scenarios and strategies for how to deal with them. They should ask, "What are our nightmares about working together?" he says. Issues that often come up include who should make quick decisions when necessary, procedures to handle sudden surprises, and establishing the general level of trust among team members. "Then I ask teams to invent some procedural ground rules. I've seen teams do exercises where the members just declare that they'll trust one another. It rarely works."

Stick to the Facts

One good way to keep conflict productive and impersonal is to focus on the facts. "The reason conflict happens is that people have the same data and interpret it differently, or they have different data in the first place," says Robbins.

In their book *Difficult Conversations: How to Discuss What Matters Most,* authors Douglas Stone, Bruce Patton, and Sheila Heen define three underlying conversations that influence people during a heated debate: The "what happened?" conversation, the "feelings" conversation, and the "identity" conversation. These internal dialogues influence the direction of conflict. The authors' advice? Tackle each conversation individually. Explore what happened. Too often, people assume they understand the other person's position. Don't go on assumptions, but rather paraphrase what the other person is saying. That simple exercise can clear up misconceptions and make your conversation partner more open to your side of the story, says Hennessey.

Find a Time and a Place for Conflict

Conflict is most dangerous when it lurks under the surface. Scud e-mails and water cooler politics will slowly erode a team's ability to function. The character of the people on your team will partially determine how much of this behavior goes on, but there are also methods you can use to discourage it.

Some experts suggest setting special times and places to address issues. That can take the form of regularly scheduled meetings to air grievances or disagreements, or it can be limited to a particular room. But be careful. "You can say: 'room three is the conflict room.' But you have to be careful about doing it that way, because when they go into room three for some unrelated purpose, people will go into conflict mode unconsciously," says Robbins.

It's also easier to manage conflict when the team members know each other on a personal level. Leaders can facilitate that by getting team members to spend time with each other away from the work environment. But that doesn't mean requiring everyone to show up at a company picnic. Instead, says Robbins, "say something like 'hey, let's take the afternoon off and see a movie.' If done carefully, it can really go a long way towards getting people used to each other as human beings and allies."

Another way to get team members used to one another is to ask each to give a three-minute personal and professional update at the beginning of meetings. "This builds relationships before the meeting gets into content—it has an amazing effect on the communication that follows," says Shechtman.

Finally, don't let anyone force the issue before it's time to make a decision. A key hallmark of destructive conflict is the call to take sides, even before a decision is really necessary. "You're with me on this, Tom, aren't you?" is a common refrain in team meetings or at water coolers. But often such pleas for support come before the options have been weighed, and before everyone has had their say. And when issues are forced before everyone has contributed, resentment builds. Instead, say, "let's talk about the facts we're discussing and find out what the group consensus is."

Lead by Example

The team members' personalities and the ground rules you put in place can have an impact on the effectiveness of conflict, but there is another important factor—the behavior of the team leader.

Practice Full Disclosure

In an argument or discussion, team members should reveal all of their arguments and make it clear why they have taken a particular position. This behavior should start at the top. "The least effective leaders are opaque—no one knows anything about them. They're kind of like mythological figures," says Shechtman. "To get people to trust you, you have to be transparent. There has to be risk up front to get feedback and manage conflict, and that starts with self-disclosure."

Make It a Learning Experience

When things go wrong, look at the situation as a learning experience rather than an opportunity to point fingers. Your example will influence members of the team to behave the same way. "Encourage an exploration of the causes of the failure, and what could be changed next time. Make the process remedial rather than punitive. If you set a solution orientation, you're saying to people: even if one person is right and the other wrong, the reality is that this is just about learning," says Robbins.

Be Seen, Not Heard

"The leader's listening-to-telling ratio should be 90 to 10," says Shechtman. Instead of making decisions, be the facilitator. When you do speak up, restate team members' arguments and positions, and encourage people in disagreement to do the same. That exercise points out discrepancies in underlying assumptions or interpretations that could send disagreements spiraling into personal conflict.

Intercede When It Turns Personal

When conflict between team members does get personal, it's time to get involved. "As a team leader, I might facilitate a conversation if it's taking a long time to get to a resolution. I will spend time with each party to figure out what is making it so difficult for them, to give them a different angle on the problem," says Weiss. If that doesn't work, the best choice may be to find a mediator—perhaps someone from a different department—who has no stake in the outcome.

What you're really shooting for is self-governance, says Guttman. Once team members learn to handle difficulties themselves, they'll work out conflicts more efficiently, and disagreements will be aired at the conference table instead of around the water cooler.

Old-school conflict avoidance tended to push conflict under the table, but times are changing. "In the past, teams were supposed to be about backslapping and feeling good," says Shechtman. But the new economy demands otherwise. "Team members should challenge each other to grow and treat each other as resilient."

For Further Reading

Communication Skills for Surviving Conflicts at Work by Janice Walker Anderson, Myrna Foster-Kuehn, and Bruce Converse McKinney (1999, Hampton Press, 187 pp.)

Difficult Conversations: How to Discuss What Matters Most by Douglas Stone, Bruce Patton, and Sheila Heen (2000, Penguin, 272 pp.)

"'I Just Can't Bring Myself to Talk About That with Her': How to have the difficult conversations and keep them productive" (*Harvard Management Communication Letter*, March 2000, Reprint C0003B)

Reprint C0007A

Handling Conflict in Teams

A Roundup of Recent Research

• • •

Managers hate it, but it's inevitable in today's time-stressed, under-peopled companies: interpersonal conflicts happen, and they must be dealt with. Recent research yields some clues as to how to defuse the tensions. Armed with some tactics for dealing with recognizable, difficult personality types, managers can approach the next team meeting with less dread and more purpose.

Avoid 'Tit for Tat' Reactions

One of the most common mistakes managers make is to respond in kind to disruptive behavior in teams. If Fred explodes at a coworker, it's tempting to yell back at him, "Settle down!" But this reaction only escalates the problem. Moreover, it reinforces Fred's behavior—he got the reaction he wanted. Instead, try to respond in an unexpected way: change the subject, the tone, or the direction

> If one member of your team misbehaves, explore the possibility that she is signaling deeper problems within the team.

of the meeting. You'll throw Fred off balance and lessen the likelihood that he'll try his tactic again. You may also acknowledge the underlying anger—calmly—and request a change in behavior. "I see you're very upset about this, Fred, but I think we could deal with the issue better if you would calm down. Please, sit down, stop pounding the table, and settle down."

Look for the Underlying Message

It's a truism in family therapy that the child who's brought to see the therapist for misbehavior is merely the weak link in a chain of family unhappiness. Similarly, if one member of your team misbehaves, explore the possibility that she is signaling deeper problems within the team. Of course, it's also possible that the team member is simply a jerk. But it's wise to take the time to search out other, deeper possible causes for the unhappiness.

Use the Team to Heal the Team

The temptation for managers in charge of the group dynamics is to enforce solutions using the personal authority of the leader. But you should employ this tactic with care. Solutions imposed from on high tend not to be as thorough and lasting as solutions that the team arrives at itself. First, give the team a chance to work out its own problems. Use the team's need to achieve its common goals as a way of pointing it toward a solution.

Lose the Battle; Win the War

Managers must always balance short-term benefit against long-term need. The equation is especially critical in building effective teams. Before you crush the misbehavior of one individual in the interests of getting immediate results, weigh how important the long-term participation of that individual is to your team. It may be wise to accept some short-term pain in order to build long-term strength and trust.

How to Satisfy the Show-Off

Every team has them: the folks who need to hear themselves talk and to constantly trumpet their own successes. It's best to give the show-off something of what he needs. Offer some compliments to this tiresome individual as soon as he pauses for breath. Then, switch the attention to someone else. "Bill, that really worked well for you; what have you found successful, Lisa?"

How to Calm the Eager Beaver

They remind you of puppy dogs, the team members who are always positive, always anxious to please, and finally annoying because of their very efforts not to be. The best way to deal with these helpful people is to praise them for their constant contribution and ask someone else to take a turn. "Bob, you're really pulling your weight here; Jane, what can you offer us in this instance?"

How to Silence the Heckler

There are days when you'd like to shoot these folks: the people who interrupt every brainstorming session with criticism, analysis of the flaws of all the suggestions on the table, and general disapproval of all the options. The only way to deter this irritating type is to challenge her to come up with something positive: "Sue, you've made it very clear why you think these ideas won't work. What do you think will work?"

How to Sound Out the Sotto Voce

Remember the kid who sat in the back of the class and made sarcastic remarks about everything the teacher said, in a voice quiet enough that the teacher usually missed the comment? Deal with it in the same way the clever teacher did: "I'm sorry, John, I didn't catch that comment. Can you repeat it, please? I don't like to miss anyone's contribution." Most of the team will be on your side, recognizing the destructive nature of the whispering campaign, and will be glad to have it stopped.

How to Move the Mule

Most teams have them: characters who just don't want anything to change. If their concerns are real, you must deal with them. But there also comes a time when a team must take action, period. In that case, give the slowpoke another course of action: offer to take the issue up with a senior executive (having previously cleared the matter with the VIP) or send the naysayer off on a separate project of his own.

How to Realign the Right but Irrelevant Ringer

There are always people with pet issues, causes, or needs that simply won't be silenced. They go on and on down a road that has little to do with the path you are trying to follow. Here, you'll need to be assertive. Take the blame on yourself and redirect the conversation. "I'm sorry, Ed.

91

I must have defined that issue poorly. What we're really talking about here is this. . . ."

When confronted with behavior that disrupts the smooth working of your team, acknowledge the underlying emotion or issue beneath the behavior, while requesting that the behavior stop. You'll find that dealing with the legitimate deeper issues will remove the need for the aberrant behavior in the long run.

For Further Reading

Communication Skills for Surviving Conflicts at Work by Janice Walker Anderson, Myrna Foster-Kuehn, and Bruce Converse McKinney (1999, Hampton Press, 187 pp.)

Reprint C0004F

Why the Members of Your Team Won't Speak Up, and What You Can Do About It

. . .

Mattison Crowe

At a time when a growing number of businesses rely on teams as their chief tool for change, managers necessarily feel a need to better understand team dynamics. Research suggests they still have a lot to learn. In a study of 179 companies by the Mercer Management consulting firm, 69% of those who used teams extensively said they planned to increase their reliance on teams in the next three years. Yet only 23 of the 179 companies were determined by the study's authors to have excellent cross-functional teams. Why were the other 156 unable to attain the same results? Work by Professors Paul Mulvey of North Carolina State University, John Veiga of the University of Connecticut, and Priscilla Elsass of Clark University points to at least one possible reason—team members are unable to disagree effectively.

Causes for Withdrawal

Mulvey, Veiga, and Elsass interviewed 569 managers to find out what caused them to withdraw from the decision-making process and team discussions. The six most common causes were as follows, ranked in descending order of frequency.

1. The Presence of Someone with Expertise

Actually, there need not be an expert present; the group has only to think that one is. When team members feel someone else has a great deal of background on an issue or problem, their natural reaction may well be to give their proxy to the expert.

Unfortunately, their decision overlooks the fact that even the best experts retain individual biases which can render flawed solutions.

2. The Presentation of a Compelling, but Inferior Argument

Stephen Covey and others have noted that the enemy of the "best" is the "good"—meaning that while people rarely have trouble deciding between alternatives labeled good and bad, they have much more difficulty differentiating the best from what is merely good. Faced with discussions that seem to go nowhere, the team may accept a plausible solution to a problem rather than probing in pursuit of other, possibly better solutions.

3. Lack of Confidence in Their Ability to Contribute

Recent newcomers may be unfamiliar with the types of problems the team normally confronts, making them less likely to participate. But don't assume that tenure guarantees involvement: Without the right kinds of encouragement, even seasoned team members may never develop the confidence required to make their views known.

4. The Decision to Be Made Seems Unimportant or Meaningless

If members feel an issue has little bearing on their particular work unit, they are more likely not to offer input to alter the team's direction. The situation can deteriorate to the point where members voice only concerns that come strictly off their own agendas. Meetings become more efficient, but less effective.

5. Pressures from Others to Conform to the Team's Decision

Reaching consensus does not always mean achieving complete agreement. Sometimes, though, pressure to achieve unanimous support for an idea can begin early in the process and, as the need to demonstrate progress grows, become progressively more intense. The team may even unwittingly appoint a gatekeeper or "defender of unanimity" whose role is to protect the group from disturbing thoughts or ideas.

6. There's a Dysfunctional Decision-Making Climate

During the formative stages of the group's work, team members may get signals that others are experiencing frustration, indifference, or disorganization. This is natural, since tasks and responsibilities have yet to be refined. But some members may take this confusion as a cue to limit their involvement.

What to Do

So how do you, as team leader, teach others the art of participation, or, even more important, of dissent? How can you solicit opposing viewpoints in a way that invites dialogue and produces a superior decision? In general, what you have to overcome is the perception of disagreement as *reactive*—people seeing others responding to their ideas and interpreting that as personal confrontation. Your challenge is to make the discussion as *proactive* as possible. From the outset, try to instill a nonthreatening feel to the team's deliberations. The most obvious step is to ask people for their opinions, and then to recognize their contributions with praise or other encouragement. It may help, too, to have an open discussion of what makes teams effective, and what hinders them. But there are other, less obvious steps that you can take as well.

Clarify the Objectives You and Others Are Working Toward

"Begin by asking members to define what their priority is in the situation," recommends Andrzej Huczynski, a senior lecturer at the University of Glasgow Business School. "Next," he advises, "list what has already been done towards achieving that stated goal. Then highlight the gap or difference between the two, based on the information you have obtained." Arguing about tactics is a waste of time if people don't share the same objectives. Write them down if you have to, but make sure they are shared and acknowledged before you roll up your sleeves. With objectives clearly outlined, you always have a secure platform of consensus to fall back on if the confrontation becomes too intense. Another benefit of writing objectives down is that it provides shy team members with an opportunity to submit ideas without the threat of having to express them aloud.

How to Tell if Your Team's at Risk

You suspect that members of the group have concerns they're not voicing, but you're not sure. According to *The Abilene Paradox: Management of Agreement* by J. B. Harvey, if any of the following situations obtain, you're probably right:

- There's conflict within the organization. Group members seem to feel frustrated, impotent, and unhappy when trying to deal with it. They may avoid meetings at which the conflict is being discussed, even to the extent of trying to spend as much time as possible away from the office. Or they may be looking for other jobs.
- Team members place much of the blame for the dilemma on the boss or on other groups.
- Small subgroups of friends or associates meet over coffee or lunch to discuss organizational

Offer Inquiring Points of View

Ira Chaleff, author of *The Courageous Follower,* suggests raising with the group "questions we might expect." Examples include:

"How would we respond to the concern that _____?"

"Could it appear to conflict with our values on _____?"

"How might _____ interpret that?"

problems. There's a lot of disagreement as to the cause of the troubles and the ways to solve them. Much of what's said begins with assertions like "We should do. . .".

- In meetings where team members meet with people from other groups to discuss the problem, they pull their punches, or state their positions in ambiguous terms, or even reverse these positions to suit the stances taken by others.

- You hear that after such meetings, members have complained to associates they trust that they didn't really say what they wanted to but were sure, for many reasons, that their comments or suggestions would have been unacceptable.

If this sounds like what goes on in many organizations much of the time, right again. And most people in most organizations probably aren't speaking up.

"How would we answer charges that _____?"

"What alternatives might our stakeholders want us to consider?"

"What would we say if asked about other options we considered and why they were discarded?"

Your purpose is to allow the group to shift its perspective slightly, to engage it in critically assessing the issues and to help it avoid the reflex to push back.

Appoint Yourself the Devil's Advocate

Playing the devil's advocate is a highly effective method of opposing a viewpoint because it lifts the disagreement off the personal level. Be sure that people understand that you're taking on the role, and why. You are here to open up a dialogue, to challenge assumptions and conclusions with hopes of offering alternative viewpoints for others to review. That is, after all, where much of the power of teams comes from.

After some exposure, team members may be comfortable taking on the role themselves. Let them.

Encourage Everyone to Do Their Homework

Before challenging the team's thinking, you and anyone else in the group need to have conducted due diligence—gathered supporting data, spoken to key people, and so on. Arming oneself with a cache of supporting information builds your credibility and leads to a more informed discussion.

Accept the Final Results Gracefully

Make sure you don't treat controversies as win-lose situations. This is not likely to be the last time teammates disagree among themselves—nor should you want it to be. If you solidify your reputation as someone who handles all outcomes well, others will follow your lead.

For Further Reading

"How Teams Contribute to Profitable Growth" by James Down (June 1996, *Management Review Executive Forum*)

"When teammates raise a white flag" by Paul W. Mulvey, John F. Veiga, & Priscilla M. Elsass (1996, *Academy of Management Executive*, Vol. 10, No. 1, 10 pp.)

Influencing Within Organizations: Getting In, Rising Up, Moving On by Andrzej Huczynski (1996, Prentice Hall, 300 pp.)

The Courageous Follower by Ira Chaleff (1995, Berrett-Koehler, 194 pp.)

The Abilene Paradox: Management of Agreement by Jerry B. Harvey (1974, *Organizational Dynamics*, Vol. 3, 318 pp.)

Reprint U9611C

Teams

Solving the Sophomore Slump

• • •

Rebecca M. Saunders

Most new teams—self-managing, cross-functional, whatever—start out full of energy. Members are eager to tackle the team's objectives. They get to meetings early, complete assignments on time, and stay late to discuss issues. A year or two later, the situation is different. Now members are showing up late or not at all. They're distracted during meetings. Even if the team gets some things done, it isn't anywhere near as effective as during the first year.

This problem is well known to the people who study teams for a living; it goes by the term "sophomore slump" or, sometimes, "team mid-life crisis." The good news is that it can be prevented—or if it's too late for that, treated. Experts recommend 10 key steps.

1: Set Up a "Team-Support" System

Jacalyn Sherriton, principal of Corporate Management Developers and coauthor of *Corporate Culture/Team Culture,* points out that organizations may pay lip service to the value of employees working together but fail to offer much support. Expectations for teams aren't clearly defined. There are no programs to recognize and celebrate team success, no efforts to sustain team vigor. If that's the case at your company, don't despair: you can address the problem by setting up ground rules when the team is formed. The rules, says Sherriton, might cover issues such as rotation of team members and duties, including team leadership; announcements about key milestones met; rewards for individual efforts; standards by which the team evaluates its own progress; and even the process by which a cross-functional team can decide to disband if members believe it has lost its usefulness. Adds Sherriton, "Often teams go on and on because no one has told them to stop."

2: Spotlight Team Progress

Deborah Harrington-Mackin, author of *Keeping the Team Going: A Tool Kit to Renew & Refuel Your Workplace Teams,* says that lack of interest from management can be a killer, leading team members to ask themselves, "Why are we doing this?" She suggests that a team sponsor agree from the outset to act as the team's press agent and cheerleader, announcing its accomplishments and attending periodic meetings to show support.

3: Teach Team Members New Skills

The opportunity for additional training can revitalize a team, says Florence Stone, coauthor of *The High-Value Manager: Developing the Core Competencies Your Organization Demands.* New United Motor Manufacturing Inc. (NUMMI), a plant owned jointly by General Motors and Toyota, empowers its self-directed teams to train each other as well as to determine training best suited for new hires. NUMMI, once solely a GM facility, was described by a GM manager as the "worst plant in the world." Now it is considered an exemplar of the benefits of high-performance work organization and cooperative labor relations. Says Michael J. Damer, manager of community relations and general affairs: "If teams are charged with—and responsible for—training members in the best possible way to do a job, their success is ensured."

4: Identify New Team Goals

Without suitable direction, teams can find themselves working on missions relevant to last year's corporate strategy. To avoid this, they should review their mission regularly in light of changing organizational priorities. Herman Miller, the office-furniture manufacturer, goes so far as to conduct "virtual reality" strategy sessions

> ## Lack of interest from management can be a killer.

for manufacturing workers. Employees learn the organization's needs, then create teams around new strategic initiatives. Alternatively, teams may simply have "plateaued," to use a term of Harrington-Mackin's. One pediatric nursing team she studied, for example, lost much of its enthusiasm 18 months into the process. The group had made significant improvements in productivity, scheduling, and patient care, but members were now demanding new and more challenging goals. If that's the case, it's up to the team and its sponsor to come up with new objectives.

5: Improve Team Processes and Procedures

Over time, says Stone, an author and speaker on management issues, the quality of team meetings can slide. Guidelines set at the beginning are forgotten. Meetings are run without agendas. More time is spent talking than doing. As people find themselves listening to colleagues drone on rather than getting things done, they find less reason to attend. If this is the problem, it's time to review the guidelines set at the time the group was formed. Members may want to reaffirm existing ground rules or add new ones to address the team's problems.

6: Rotate Team Assignments

Picker International manufactures health care equipment, mainly medical imaging equipment for CAT scans. "Picker relies heavily on teams and teamwork," says George W. Gotschall, manager of total quality management. "However, it was this very reliance on teams that eventually led to burnout and overburdening of team participants." Teams were formed as needed. Most had six or fewer members, so the demands on employees' time were significant. Employees quickly mastered their functions within a team, but over time the work became monotonous and they lost interest. Picker's solution: rotate members through all team functions and jobs, with assignments determined through a drawing. Says Gotschall: "Besides keeping interest level and morale high, this system acts as an informal certification system for all employees and ensures that employees are cross-trained fully on a variety of functions within production."

7: Create a Culture That Takes Teamwork Seriously

At Chaparral Steel, self-managed teams determine the materials and equipment necessary to complete a task. "Who better than our employees to determine the best way to do the job?" says VP of administration Dennis Beach, communicating the attitude that has kept Chaparral's teams energized. A similar attitude prevails at Trenton Brewery of Miller Brewing, according to human resources team manager Daniel E. Rick. Teams used to be employed for "odds and ends" functions, says Rick, undermining both members' morale and their eagerness to pursue new initiatives. Then Miller decided to organize the entire brewery around self-directed teams, making them responsible for key processes from brewing to distribution. Employees know that teams play a vital part in the brewery's operation, and enthusiasm stays high.

8: Compensate Teams for the Extra Work They Do

Team involvement usually means extra hours of work, whether in completing team assignments or simply going to meetings in addition to doing a regular job. Given the hours they spend, members expect some dollar recognition if they succeed—particularly if there's a financial side to the team's mission. If they don't get that acknowledgment, they'll be less willing to find the extra hours going into the second or third year. The more reward for participation, moreover, the more likely

> ## Sometimes a little new blood works wonders.

individuals will be to contribute. At Motorola, teams determine merit pay of individual members; they even make decisions concerning the allocation of merit pay. Most start out with merit-pay criteria based 80% on individual factors and 20% on team factors. They typically progress to a 50-50 split, the maximum allowed by the company.

9: Keep Team Members in the Loop

New teams seem to have easy access to the information they need to achieve their mission. But as attention drifts to newer initiatives, managers forget to alert team members about opportunities or warn them about challenges. Too late, members get information that would have influenced their action plans, and they begin to question their organization's interest in their efforts. If this is a problem, team leaders need to get a commitment from senior managers to ensure a steady flow of information. Herman Miller, for example, holds monthly business reviews that provide self-directed and cross-functional teams with information about corporate developments relating to product and service quality, stocks, suggestions, cost savings, and other areas.

10: Bring in Outsiders to Refresh the Team

You can rotate team duties—and you can rotate team members. Sometimes a little new blood works wonders. Harrington-Mackin, a team-management expert with Bennington, Vt.-based New Directions Management Services, also suggests that a team leader can change the dynamics of a slumping team by bringing in visitors—senior managers, for instance, or even customers. In fact, some teams may want to add a customer representative to the team itself. Meetings with other teams, either within the organization or in comparable organizations, are another way of stimulating new thinking and revitalizing the group, she says.

The bottom line? Team members don't have to suffer from boredom, frustration, or anger; there are actions that they as a group can take to correct the sophomore slump or mid-life crisis of their group. Better yet, they can prevent the problem in the first place by building an infrastructure that keeps the team vital throughout its lifetime.

For Further Reading

Building a Dynamic Team: A Practical Guide to Maximizing Team Performance by Richard Y. Chang (1994, Jossey-Bass Publishers, 105 pp.)

Building Productive Teams: An Action Guide and Resource Book by Glenn H. Varney (1989, Jossey-Bass Publishers, 170 pp.)

Compensation for Teams: How to Design and Implement Team-Based Reward Programs by Steven E. Gross (1995, AMACOM, 336 pp.)

Corporate Culture/Team Culture: Removing the Hidden Barriers to Team Success by Jacalyn Sherriton and James L. Stern (1996, AMACOM, 215 pp.)

Don't Fire Them, Fire Them Up: A Maverick's Guide to Motivating Yourself and Your Team by Frank Pacetta (1995, Fireside, 288 pp.)

40 Tools for Cross-Functional Teams: Building Synergy for Breakthrough Creativity by Walter J. Michalski (1998, Productivity Press, 165 pp.)

Keeping the Team Going: A Tool Kit to Renew & Refuel Your Workplace Teams by Deborah Harrington-Mackin (1996, AMACOM, 230 pp.)

Reprint U9907C

Managing Communication Within Diverse and Virtual Teams

• • •

Thanks to demographic trends and the advent of communication technologies, cross-generational and virtual teams have proliferated across the business landscape. Each of these types of teams poses special challenges for managers.

In this section, you'll learn about the importance of understanding different generations' unique perspectives and motivators—and adapting your communications and managerial style to each to obtain the best results. You'll also find recommendations for establishing a sharp sense of shared purpose and commitment in a virtual team—which grows even more challenging in groups whose members rarely or never meet face-to-face.

Motivating Across Generations

• • •

David Stauffer

In the 1988 movie *Big*, actor Tom Hanks portrays Josh Baskin, a Little Leaguer who, after being granted his wish to be magically transplanted into an adult body, quickly ascends the corporate ladder at a toy manufacturer because he has retained his early teen's mentality and insight.

Although *Big* stretches generational differences in the workplace beyond credibility, it nonetheless demonstrates the benefits an organization can realize by reaching across generations to tap the perspectives and talents of employees of all ages. It also demonstrates the doubts, resentments, and befuddlement that can arise from one generation's pejorative judgment of another generation's characteristic thinking and behavior.

For example, if you're a member of the Baby Boom generation (roughly age 41 to 58), you may believe members of Generation X (approximately age 24 to 40) are ego-centric slackers whose work can be supervised as easily as cats can be herded. If you're an Xer, you may perceive Boomers as staid, demanding, and about as creative and fun-loving as a stop sign.

And if you're a member of the Silent generation (roughly age 59 and older), you may cringe at the thought of re-tiring and leaving your organization in the hands of Boomers, Xers, and the newest workforce entrants, Generation Y (about 23 and younger)—because that whole conglomeration of successor generations lacks the spirit of self-sacrifice and dedication to a common cause by which you and your cohorts made your respective organizations strong.

Such age-based pigeonholing of other generations can harm your organization more today than in the past because members from many generations are mixing in the workplace more than ever before:

- Workers are increasingly staying in or re-entering the workforce after they reach traditional retirement age.

- Young workers are more quickly assuming important roles in their companies.

- Many company hierarchies have given way to team-based structures that often include people of all ages.

- Seniority counts for far less today.

"That system was simple," says Bruce Tulgan, CEO of generation consultants RainmakerThinking in New Haven, Conn. "The old were in charge and the young did what they were told. That's gone." In its place is a more complex workplace, one in which managers must be sensitive to age-related issues to be effective.

That imperative packs a one-two punch at the U.S. Equal Employment Opportunity Commission (EEOC), which not only must handle an increasing volume of age-discrimination charges, according to chair Cari M. Dominguez, but must also tend to its own internal generation mix. "Almost 40% of the EEOC workforce is retirement-eligible," Dominguez says, "a share that will jump to well more than half in the next few years. Figuring out how to blend incoming Gen Xers and Yers with Boomers and others isn't an option but a necessity."

The key implication of the mixed-generation workplace for you, the manager, is clear: The better you understand the unique combination of factors that motivates each generation, the better you can tap those motivators and gain the best combined effort from your entire team.

Accommodating Each Generation's Perspective

Members of each generation acquire their own unique motivators, attributes, and worldviews as they live through a shared set of watershed events and conditions. Only the Silents lived through formative years that included (among many other influencers) the Great Depression and World War II. Boomers experienced the assassination of President Kennedy and the Vietnam War, while the AIDS epidemic and drive-by shootings shaped Xers.

Common experience doesn't dictate common attitudes among all members of a given generation. But it does mean that people of like age tend to carry similar influences with them through their lives and careers. Thus managers can be led astray by one of their most frequently used methods of figuring out how to motivate younger people. "We think back to what we wanted when we were their age," says Claire Raines, who heads her own Denver-based generations consultancy. "That's more than unproductive; it takes us in the wrong direction." Your own experience as a manager is important, but you need to realize that it has been crucially shaped by generation-specific events and attitudes. In advocating intergenerational understanding, psychologist Hank Karp, a professor of management at Hampton University (Hampton, Va.) and a coauthor of *Bridging the Boomer-Xer Gap*, says, "I don't mean that one generation

What Tends to Motivate the Gens

No two people are best motivated in exactly the same way. But some motivators tend to be generation-based. Here's the expert consensus *Harvard Management Update* found on some generation-specific motivators.

Silents (or Veterans): Choose formality over informality. For example, communicate face-to-face and by live phone calls rather than voicemail, fax, or e-mail. Explain the logic of any action. Use traditional forms of recognition—plaques, certificates, photos with top executives.

Boomers: Lay out a clear series of steps toward a defined goal. State objectives and desired results in people-centered terms. Make Boomers part of a team effort; pep talks can help. Choose forms of recognition that are widely noticed, such as an article in the company newsletter.

Xers: Tell them what needs to get done but not how to do it. Give them multiple tasks but let them set their own priorities. Avoid platitudes and buzzwords. Provide frequent and frank feedback, and ask for their reaction and opinions. Pep talks can be a turn-off. Allow time for fun. Recognize them with bonus days off.

Yers (or Nexters): Provide opportunities for continuous learning and building skills. Know their personal goals and tell them how the tasks they've been assigned fit into those goals. Emphasize the positive; look on the bright side. Be more of a coach and less of a boss. Communicate informally—for example, through e-mail and brief hallway encounters.

has to adopt the values of the other. I don't even mean that one has to understand the values of the other." Instead, he says, peace and productivity can result from merely recognizing and allowing differing values.

Case in point: David L. Larson, professor and chair of the department of plastic surgery at the Medical College of Wisconsin (Milwaukee), and his peers found themselves increasingly troubled by the behavior and perceived attitudes of residents. "Some of us would tell a resident to do something, and he or she would question it or simply not do it," says Larson. "We sensed different values. Some residents bluntly told their directors to chill out—that they worked too hard."

Larson brought in Raines to provide some training about generational differences. It paid off when Larson issued a seemingly minor change in the residents' on-call hospital coverage. "The reaction was a firestorm of protest. Before the training, I'd have come down with an iron fist. Instead, I called a meeting of all the residents. We discussed the schedule and how I'd announced it. After 30 minutes, they said, 'That's cool.' The agreed schedule was no different from the one I'd announced. But the residents were included in the process of coming up with it."

On the Team

The generational divide isn't so stark in many workplaces. This makes it even harder to recognize conflict that may be generation-based, says Raines. "When we're growing up, our own generational characteristics are no more visible than the air we breathe. So, after we move into the workforce and begin to supervise others, we tend not to regard remarks like 'He's not a team player' as generation-based. But they usually are."

> Managers can be led astray by one of their most frequently used ways to figure out how to motivate younger people.

A need to feel part of a team is a common value among Boomers but a rarer one among Gen Xers and Yers. This doesn't mean Xers and Yers can't be motivated; rather, they're more likely to be motivated by a call for independent action than for a team effort. The team effort most Boomers envision, Raines says, is more like football, in which every member acts in concert. For Gen X, it's more like a relay race: "I'll give it all I've got—when and where I'm supposed to."

Imposing the values of one's own generation on others is alarmingly easy, says Wally Doolin, CEO of the

About Those Disillusioned Boomers

Today's advice to managers on generation-based motivation may tend to be addressed to Boomers as bosses
and dwell on Xers as subordinates. That makes sense, as
the current age ranges of Boomers and Xers are such
that the former generation would likely predominate
among all bosses and the latter would be the most
prevalent generation among subordinates. Nonetheless,
with some 58 million Boomers in the U.S. civilian non-
institutional workforce—representing more than 40% of
all such American workers (according to generation consultants RainmakerThinking)—the largest-ever generation has millions of its members in subordinate positions.

They represent a special challenge to supervisors, perhaps not so much because many bosses will be younger
than a Boomer subordinate but more because many of
these subordinates may be discouraged or disillusioned
about work. Origins of this unhappiness lie in the U.S.
economic downturn of the late 1980s and early 1990s,
says Beverly Goldberg, a vice president of The Century
Foundation (New York City) and author of *Age Works:
What Corporate America Must Do to Survive the Graying of
the Workforce* (Free Press, 2000). "These people felt very
much abandoned," she says.

Disillusioned Boomers may be more prevalent in the
workforce than disgruntled Xers, not just owing to
Boomers' sheer numbers or adverse experiences, but to
one of their defining generational traits: Job loyalty.
Boomers tend to feel a greater obligation of loyalty,
which can extend to sticking with an unhappy work situation. Additionally, says psychologist Hank Karp,

Boomers tend to hang on to jobs because of economic dependence and a need for security. His research has consistently found that if you have a typical Boomer and a typical Xer, both of whom are unhappy in their work, under the same economic conditions "the Xer will be more likely to quit and the Boomer more likely to stay," he says.

That presents a tough motivational task for employers, but many companies only demotivate the Boomers further, says Goldberg. "Often the company doesn't give them training because it's thought [the Boomers] aren't going to stay long. There's an aura of silence that surrounds employees who are pushed to the side of an organization. But it's important to keep these people trained and informed." Keep these Boomers up to date with essential technology skills, such as using the Web effectively. And practice what Goldberg terms "age ergonomics," for example, with a flexible schedule that excuses lateness on snow days and switches hours to allow early departures to avoid driving after dark, or provide computers for employees to use at home when necessary.

Make extra efforts to include plateaued Boomers on special committees not concerned with regular job duties, such as those related to emergency planning or philanthropic activities. "Such involvement helps them feel they're learning new things, broadening themselves, and preparing for the future," Goldberg says. That's motivational in simultaneously responding to two major concerns of an older employee: Will I have enough money to retire? and What will I do during my retirement years?

Dallas-based national restaurant chain la Madeleine French Bakery and Café. "It's easy to think, 'Why don't they do things the way I do things?' One of my general managers, a real do-it-yourself Boomer, told me, 'I just can't get it. These [young] people aren't willing to do what we need them to do.'" Later, she told him that a seminar on managing younger workers helped her. "But it will probably take continual development for her and the other GMs, because their job is so much tougher today," he says.

"Most of today's employees don't respond to traditional motivators," says RainmakerThinking's Tulgan. "So managing is much more of a high-maintenance undertaking." The awareness of differing generational values that Doolin's GM acquired is often the first step. It's almost certain to enhance self-awareness as well. "I learned a lot about my own generation as well as others," says Dominguez. "I thought, 'No wonder we're like this!'"

A smart next step is sharing that awareness with your team. "One of the best things a manager can do is have a general discussion" about motivation, says Raines. A flatter organizational structure may better accommodate such a discussion and ongoing cross- generational motivation. "With a flatter organization, you don't have so much overt competition among coworkers to move up," says Connie Fuller, human resources manager for the Genoa, Ill., manufacturing facility of Lucent Technologies' subsidiary AG Communication Systems and a coauthor of *Bridging the Boomer-Xer Gap*.

"Most important, though, is continual training and development, and the flexibility for people to try new roles," she continues. "When I talk about those aspects of teams, young people nod their heads. They have no illusion of cradle-to-grave employment. They feel they have to take care of themselves. The manager who thinks that finding ways to motivate these people is an exciting challenge will be among the best managers, not just of generational diversity, but all diversity."

Looking Past the "Clutter"

How can a manager address all the forms of diversity—racial, ethnic, gender, and religious—that Fuller refers to? "That points to a customized approach to each of your people," says Tulgan. "Managing people ultimately involves an ongoing conversation about two issues: First, what can I do for you? Second, here's what I need from you." Generational considerations, as well as issues around other forms of diversity, can help a manager in this conversation. "I make broad generalizations about age cohorts all the time," Tulgan says, as others do about other individual attributes. "These generalizations are nothing more than a guide—a lens through which you can view people so you can understand them better and work with them more effectively. The most successful managers are those who know the limits of the lens. They create as many career paths as they have employees."

For Raines, this means uncovering characteristics without judging them. "It all comes down to casting aside our tendency to make judgments," she says. Tera Sunder, a Dallas recruiting manager for Starbucks (Seattle), concurs. "We all have biases," she says. "The challenge is to realize them and not turn them into prejudice." The job applicant who wears an oversized shirt hanging out over a pair of baggy pants, she explains, "may be thinking, 'My outfit is in style and is my best,' while you're thinking, 'What was he thinking?'" That's the sort of clutter, from each person's perspective, "that has to be eliminated so you can more clearly see the whole person."

The rewards of doing that across generations can be considerable, says EEOC Chair Dominguez. "When you understand the characteristics and uniqueness of the generations, you reduce the likelihood of legal and enforcement issues. You also ease workplace tensions and gain a stronger, more effective working relationship among all generations. Organizations that are built to last do that."

For Further Reading

Bridging the Boomer-Xer Gap: Creating Authentic Teams for High Performance at Work by Hank Karp, Connie Fuller, and Danilo Sirias (2002, Davies-Black)

Managing the Generation Mix: From Collision to Collaboration by Carolyn A. Martin and Bruce Tulgan (2002, HRD Press)

Generations at Work: Managing the Clash of Veterans, Boomers, Xers, and Nexters in Your Workplace by Ron Zemke, Claire Raines, and Bob Filipczak (1999, AMACOM)

Reprint U0303B

Virtual Teams

Paleolithic Insights About the
Art of Cyber-Managing

* * *

Some days, your direct reports act like Neanderthals—
that's because, in a manner of speaking, they are. Indeed,
we've all inherited tendencies from the earliest days of
human culture. But managers often forget the formative
influence these ancient preferences have on current group
dynamics, and that includes the most technologically
advanced of Internet Age–groups, the virtual team.

The virtual team signals "a sharp uptick in the human
capability to group," write Jessica Lipnack and Jeffrey
Stamps in *Virtual Teams*. But the Web technology that
allows far-flung colleagues to "work interdependently with
a shared purpose across space, time, and organization
boundaries" is not the most important aspect of a virtual team, maintain the authors, who are also directors

of the West Newton, Mass.- based consulting firm NetAge. In fact, says Lipnack, it's the age-old human grouping tendencies that really "make virtual teams sing." So understanding those tendencies—not getting the technology piece right—should be the first order of business for any manager charged with setting up a virtual team.

"There are some companies doing it well and perhaps 20 times that number doing it badly," Lipnack continues. The ones that excel at managing virtual teams—she cites Buckman Laboratories (Memphis, Tenn.) and Eastman Chemical (Kingsport, Tenn.)—pay careful attention to three interrelated issues: purpose, shared leadership, and communication.

1: Purpose Shapes Function and Structure

Humans have always formed groups for specific purposes, says Lipnack: they would come together to collaborate and isolated themselves to concentrate. "When you think back to the beginning of human work, hunting and gathering happened in small bands of family groups. Those were the first teams. Through the cycle of seasons, small groups would come together into larger family kinship networks, share the harvest, and go off in individual groups again when food got scarce."

A governing purpose remains the foundation of successful group collaboration today. "Purpose is the campfire around which virtual team members gather," write

Lipnack and Stamps. Roger K. Mowen, Jr., vice president and chief information officer of Eastman Chemical, concurs. "Teams do not possess magical powers to suddenly solve fuzzy, intractable issues," he declares—they need a clear purpose in order to function.

> ## With virtual teams, the boundaries are porous.

How can you imbue a virtual team with a strong sense of purpose? Work to build consensus about the following, advise Lipnack and Stamps:

Vision, "a compelling picture of the achievable, highly desired future";

Mission, a "simple statement of what the group does";

Goals, targets that translate the vision and mission into "palpable, practical results"; and

Tasks that "specify the actions that members take."

A clear purpose also helps inform your thinking about the optimal size and configuration of your virtual team. But what's interesting, observes Lipnack, is that "the same numbers that have been there since the beginning of time seem to be the natural ways in which we organize."

The typical Stone Age family, she and Stamps write, "yoked together between four and seven people as its basic socio-economic unit. . . . From time immemorial, these small units naturally congregated into larger associations" of four to six families. Now fast-forward to today: "Small teams have five to seven people, with an upper limit of 25," says Lipnack, "at which point you stop being able to have meaningful conversation around the same table."

With a virtual team, however, the optimal size is not a function of physical limitations on how many people can be present. "Size depends first on the task at hand and second on the unique constraints and opportunities of the situation," Lipnack and Stamps write. Even so, they believe that "more than 25 people on a core distributed team leads to a loss of intimacy required to sustain meaningful communication."

2: Leadership Rotates According to the Task at Hand

Paleolithic societies pooled their human capital—their knowledge about animals, the weather, and the landscape, as well as their ability to procure food and care for their young—simply in order to survive, says Lipnack. People had "different roles that had to be respected for everything to get done. Depending on what needed to get done, one or another person was the lead, so leadership shifted naturally depending on the task."

Don't Give the People Issues Short Shrift

"It doesn't matter how good the gizmo is," says Carol Willett, the executive vice president in charge of training at Applied Knowledge Group (Reston, Va.). "You can't overcome six million years of evolution." When putting together a virtual team, give human dynamics at least as high a priority as technological concerns. Work through the following four questions with your team, Willett recommends:

1: What's in It for Me?

"I've never found any group willing to collaborate unless they see a darn good reason to do so," says Willett. One suggestion: ask team members to complete the sentence, *The one thing that would make it worthwhile for me to be a member is. . . .*

2: What Constitutes Trust?

"Face to face, we trust people based on more details than we're even aware of," Willett notes. Perhaps it's a firm handshake, or looking the person in the eye. "In a virtual environmental, there's a higher potential for misunderstanding—for assuming, absent other information, that people intend to let us down." Try to get virtual team members to spell out what trust means to each of them. For example, for some people, "trust may mean that if you send me an e-mail and ask for something immediately, I'll do everything possible to get back to you in three hours or let you know why I can't."

3: What Are Our Expectations of Each Other?

"Think about a tribe," Willett recommends. "We have inbred notions of what a leader is, what a medicine man is. Virtual teams have roles, too. Somebody might be the facilitator of group discussion. Somebody else might take responsibility for bringing up to speed members who've been traveling." Because people assume more independence when they're working virtually, however, "there's more potential to get crossways with one another." So it's important to nail down the critical roles right from the start—that is, to be clear about who's handling them.

4: How Will We Share Information?

This is essentially a communication issue, not a technological one. Ask team members about their preferences related to the various technologies the group will be using—e-mail, voicemail, videoconferencing, etc.—and agree upon protocols for each.

This behavior is still relevant today. Individuals' literal survival may not depend on the success of virtual teams, as was the case with Stone Age teams. But for some firms, corporate success—if not survival—is increasingly tied to the performance of virtual teams.

"Most virtual teams have formal appointed leaders, but that doesn't mean there can't be fluid leadership." In fact, she and Stamps write, the leadership structure "as a whole is an inclusive set of related roles of leaders and followers." Leadership responsibilities break down into two categories:

Task leadership deals with "expertise, activities, and decisions required to accomplish results."

Social leadership addresses issues that "arise from interactions that generate feelings of group identity, status, attractiveness, and personal satisfaction."

3: Constant Communication Fosters a Sense of Identity

Even though a person's area of expertise typically defines her role on a task-oriented virtual team, managers ignore the social leadership functions—and especially issues related to communication and trust—at their peril.

"When access to a physical place governs availability of information, the whole group can watch as new members transition into full participants through their rites of passage," write Lipnack and Stamps. But with virtual teams, the boundaries are porous: "new members can instantly gain access to all of the group's information," thereby weakening traditional patterns of socialization. Thus an inclusive environment and plentiful communication become increasingly important tools for building group identity. They give virtual team members "the feeling that they can participate," explains Lipnack.

"They're essential for building trust, out of which strong relationships grow."

The real business payoff comes from these trusting relationships, says Bob Buckman, former chairman and CEO of Buckman Labs' holding company, and now chairman of the consulting firm Applied Knowledge Group (Reston, Va.): "A culture of trust is absolutely essential if you want proactive knowledge sharing across time and space." Eastman Chemical's Mowen echoes the thought: improved communication, participation, and understanding in teams, he says, "are the basis for the faster learning—and faster dissemination of that learning—that we've been able to achieve."

Granted, teams that are separated in time and by geographical distance pose challenges that are unique to our age. But managing these challenges—and unleashing the distinctive potential that virtual teams possess—is best accomplished by giving first priority to the age-old forces that govern how and why humans collaborate.

For Further Reading

Virtual Teams: People Working Across Boundaries with Technology by Jessica Lipnack and Jeffrey Stamps (2000, John Wiley & Sons)

Reprint U0103C

The Art of Managing Virtual Teams

Eight Key Lessons

. . .

Charles Wardell

A company's ability to seize an opportunity often depends on how fast it can field a team of talented individuals, wherever they may be. That puts a big premium on the skills of *virtual management*—the ability to run a team whose members aren't in the same location, don't report to you, and may not even work for your organization.

So far, savvy virtual managers are rare. "I'd be surprised if anyone has it figured out yet," says Tom Kunz, a principal with Shell Oil Co.'s Network Learning and Support Center in Houston, a unit that supports the corporation's virtual projects. Royal Dutch Shell—Shell Oil's parent— has many project teams worldwide, involving people from different departments, different companies (such as joint-venture partners), and different countries. It has yet to nail down a methodology for managing them.

But though the skills are still scarce, the subject is being well studied; in fact, there's already a body of research on the keys to successful virtual management.

1: Walk Before You Run

Companies often forget that someone who can't manage a conventional team effectively probably can't handle a virtual one, either. You've got to "do successful teaming in your own house first," says Bill Hanson, a former VP of manufacturing at Digital Equipment Corporation who now is industry codirector of the Leaders for Manufacturing program at Massachusetts Institute of Technology. Success with any team means learning to make team members a top priority. "Managers have always talked about managing people, when in reality they've usually ended up managing the budget," notes George Metes, president of Virtual Learning Systems, of Manchester, N.H., a company that trains virtual teams. "In the technology age, paradoxically, you have to spend more time managing people than in the past."

2: Light a "Fire in the Belly"

A virtual team needs a clear mission. That's a major point of *Virtual Teams,* by Jessica Lipnack and Jeffrey Stamps, a book that shows managers how to create and maintain effective work relationships among geographically dispersed people. Teams that fail, says Lipnack, usually do so because they lack a clear purpose. The team must flesh out exactly what it will accomplish and how it will do so. The process works best when everyone gets involved—which often means getting together for a kickoff meeting. "You want a fire in the belly of everyone in a distributed project," says Lipnack. "We've found that the most successful teams come together at least at the beginning."

3: Assume Nothing; Spell Out Everything

In a prior assignment, Kunz spent six months collaborating on a project with Royal Dutch Shell. He describes the end of the project as "a train wreck." His Houston group's policy was to bill for its time. The unit in London assumed it wouldn't be billed for what it saw as corporate support. "They were happy with our work," recalls

Kunz, "but when we presented them with our $50,000 bill at the end of the project, they became unhappy."

You have to test assumptions about everything: how the team will communicate, what terms such as "quality" mean in practice, even whether the schedule means the same thing to everybody. Metes, of Virtual Learning Systems, recently attended a meeting of a virtual team that was late shipping a software product. After much debate, everyone agreed on a revised ship date. But just as the meeting was adjourning, a Scottish voice came over the audio asking whether that meant customers would begin getting the product on this date. A surprised developer answered that he was simply agreeing to beta-test the product on that date. "Assumptions kill," says Metes.

4: Megacommunicate

Once a project is underway, the manager has to keep team members from becoming isolated. "You need to touch the virtual team every day," says MIT's Hanson. That could mean sending e-mail, posting to a project Web site, sending faxes, or making phone calls. The manager should also encourage team members to keep in touch with one another, even when there's no pressing need to do so. Familiarity breeds trust, and people who trust one another will inevitably produce more.

The value of trust was an important finding of the Global Virtual Team project, an annual study led by Sirkka

Jarvenpaa, a professor at the University of Texas. During the 1997 study, faculty and students from universities around the world collaborated for eight weeks on a software development project, communicating only by e-mail. Jarvenpaa concluded that if team members don't meet in person at the outset, they should at least exchange get-acquainted messages. Teams that did so had more overall communication during the project. They regularly discussed goals and schedules, helped one another meet them, were quicker to confront nonperformers, and were more likely to get their work done on time.

Of course e-mail wasn't the only thing distinguishing these high-trust teams. Their managers also worked hard to clarify objectives and make sure everyone understood his or her place on the team. This created a stable atmosphere in which team members could build working relationships. The better the relationships, the more work members accomplished together. "If there's only one investment to make, make it an investment in social capital," advises Lipnack.

5: Find Allies

A common problem with virtual teams: members often work on more than one team at a time, so you may be competing with others for an individual's time. "As a team leader, you have to manage up," says Lipnack, meaning that you have to forge alliances with your team members' other managers. Ken Campbell, a senior consultant with Genesis Consulting in Ridgefield, Conn., who has served on several virtual teams, suggests getting an "executive sponsor." Suppose you need the company's legal department—500 miles away—to lend you a day of a researcher's time. You may need an alliance with someone high enough in the organization to go to the executive running that department and request help on your behalf. Be aware, though, that you're asking the higher-up for a real commitment. "The sponsor has to be willing to take phone calls on nights and weekends, if necessary," cautions Campbell. "And sponsors have to be willing to put you on their calendars at regular intervals."

6: Compensate Creatively

In a team including people from different companies, chances are that compensation will be tied to project success. Campbell suggests basing incentives on both project and personal performance (see "How to Compensate Teams," *Harvard Management Update,* November 1997). Above all, be prepared to answer the question, "If I turn in excellent work on time and ahead of schedule but the project still fails, will I get a bonus?" Of course, compensation involves more than money, and involvement in a virtual team may bring different benefits to different members. "Creating a successful product will benefit members of the corporation," says Hanson. "But what if the team includes R&D people from a university? What benefit do they get?" He suggests asking all team members at the outset to say what they want out of the project.

7: Watch for Conflict—and Learn to Manage It

Conflict is inevitable, in virtual teams as well as in conventional ones. Metes suggests keeping a constant eye out for it and taking pains to nip it in the bud. If you have an e-mail archive, check it daily for disagreements among team members. If you find any, call them in person. "A voice works better than an e-mail."

Phone conversations are a good time to probe for potential problems. "You have to have a sensitive ear and be very precise with the questions you ask people," says Genesis vice president Hal Tragash. It can be hard to hear a cry for help from an overburdened team member, and if you miss it, you could have problems down the line. "Even after a team member agrees to something, you have to test her comfort level with it by asking things like 'Are you OK with that?'"

On large, long-term teams, consider designating a "circuit rider." Metes, like Hanson, worked at Digital Equipment during the 1980s. On one large project that included teams in the U.S. and Europe, he employed a form of shuttle diplomacy, in which a team member would be designated to go from site to site listening to gripes from employees. "We used the circuit rider to explain to the Germans what the French were doing."

8: Do Better Next Time

Kunz, of Shell, has begun doing detailed postmortems of the teams he works with. "We try to bring all the parts together so everyone can see the value of their individual pieces," he says. The goal: better performance next time around. This learning from experience is particularly valuable in the oil business because so much of the work—building drilling platforms and pipelines, for example—is repetitive. But he believes that virtual workers need to understand how their parts fit into the big picture regardless of the industry.

Done well, in fact, virtual teaming can be a constant source of learning. And the lessons go beyond the virtual: Metes finds that the communication and planning skills it requires carry over to other tasks. "Once people have done it, they work colocated better."

For Further Reading

Virtual Teams: Reaching Across Space, Time, and Organizations with Technology by Jessica Lipnack and Jeffrey Stamps (1997, John Wiley & Sons, 256 pp.)

"Virtual Teams: Technology and the Workplace of the Future" by Anthony M. Townsend, Samuel M. DeMarie, and Anthony R. Hendrickson (*Academy of Management Executive*, August 1998.)

"Managing Virtual Teams: An Advanced Online Workshop" (Virtual Learning Systems, Inc.)

Reprint U9811B

Compensating and Rewarding Your Team

• • •

The most committed and competent team isn't likely to achieve top-notch performance for long if you don't compensate them for excellence. But like other aspects of managing teams, compensation and reward systems require some creative thinking. The best systems combine cash and noncash awards linked to team goals and collective achievement.

Effective compensation systems also reflect the *type* of team in question. The articles in this section explain how to adapt rewards to three team types to encourage the best performance. You'll also discover tips for offering numerous forms of cash and noncash awards.

How to Compensate Teams

• • •

Loren Gary

As in football, so in business: These days, everything is "the team, the team, the team." The power of teams is now reflexively tapped to solve just about every management problem under the sun: improving quality, integrating marketing goals into new product design, reducing the length of product development cycles, reducing absenteeism and turnover, managing costs, outsourcing payroll functions, and more.

Those lucky folk who are paid to sit around and imagine the future believe that our love affair with teams represents a key stage in the evolution of the organization. In the next century, they say, companies may consist of a series of independent mini-societies that will be cross-functional, cross-hierarchical, interdependent, and "networked." But that's tomorrow. Today, team work remains a dramatic departure from traditional approaches to getting work done. And companies have just begun to grapple with the question of how they should compensate people who work on teams.

In theory, the new team pay should tie the performance of this new work unit to a company's goals. Research suggests that "if you want people to behave as a team, you have to treat them collectively," says Edward E. Lawler III, the director of the Center for Effective Organizations at the Marshall School of Business at USC. But as compensation managers have been discovering, there is a whole different order of complexity to the design of compensation metrics for teams. That is because our existing pay systems were not made for these organisms-within-organizations that are responsible for real work. Unlike traditional work groups made up of employees reporting to the same manager, genuine teams are interdependent or mutually accountable, working together on a shared set of products, processes, and/or goals. And their members do not necessarily come from the same organizational unit.

It's also difficult for any expert to design a "one size fits all" prescription for how your company should compensate its teams because compensation systems differ widely from organization to organization. Most companies use some form of incentive pay. Steven Gross, vice president and managing director of the Hay Group in Jersey City, and author of *Compensation for Teams*, believes that, when it comes to base compensation of individuals, some systems support the work of teams more than others.

> ## Skill-based pay systems support the work of teams.

The base pay system that's most widely used is somewhat ill suited for compensating teams. Called job-based pay, it quantifies an employee's breadth of knowledge, and his or her depth of knowledge in a particular skill. The best-known job-based point system for determining salary is the Hay System, named after Ned Hay, the government worker who invented it during World War II.

The Hay System was the worldwide standard for organizational compensation until the 1980s, when downsizing, the use of technology as a competitive wedge, and global competition forced companies to invent new ways to meet their goals. But its inflexibility does not easily accommodate the fluid nature of team assignments and responsibilities. In the past decade skill-based pay has been fast replacing job-based pay as the preferred compensation system in organizations.

Roughly equivalent to knowledge-based or competency-based pay, skill-based pay determines salary according to how many skills employees have or how many jobs they can do. It encourages the employee to continuously update and acquire skills that are critical to an organization's present and future ability to compete, and is used most often by organizations in tough, competitive industries.

Some compensation experts believe that skill-based pay may be best suited to organizations that make wide use of teams because it rewards the kinds of attitudes and behaviors that make teams successful. In a 1993 article in *Compensation & Benefits*, USC's Lawler, Gerald E. Ledford, Jr., and Lei Chang wrote that skill-based pay facilitates "job rotation and cross-training, which are essential to self-managing teams."

Different Kinds of Pay for Different Kinds of Teams

Complicating the problem even further is the fact that organizational exigencies have spawned different kinds of teams. And different kinds of teams, experts believe, should be compensated differently. Ed Lawler and Susan Cohen, who is an associate professor at USC's business school, identify three kinds of teams:

- Parallel teams exist alongside the regular organizational structure, often doing problem-solving or improvement-oriented tasks. (According to one study, 85% of *Fortune* 1000 corporations use parallel teams.)

- Project teams, such as new-product development or information-systems teams, bring together knowledge workers from across disciplines to work on projects that have a definite but relatively lengthy time frame. (The workers participate full-time, until the goals are met and the team dissolves.)

- Work teams are self-contained, self-managed, interdependent units that produce a product or provide a service. (These are known as process teams; their members are full-time and membership on the team is permanent.)

While traditional compensation systems match pay to a job or a person, the challenge in compensating teams is to design a system that rewards group performance and, when appropriate, also rewards individual members of the team. Effective team-based compensation strategy uses elements of existing reward systems and tailors them to particular kinds of teams.

Compensating Parallel Teams

Because of the adjunct nature of parallel teams, Lawler and Cohen recommend compensating team members through an add-on reward system, such as a gainsharing plan, which quantifies cost reductions or other gains and, using a predetermined formula, distributes the gain among team members. While profit-sharing plans kick in quarterly or annually, gainsharing plans can take effect more quickly. They also motivate the team to generate more such ideas. Keep in mind, though, that the motivational value of the gainsharing bonus diminishes as the time draws out between the suggestion of cost-saving ideas and the award of the bonus.

Different kinds of teams require different kinds of pay.

A caveat or three: Consider offering some kind of reward to non-team members whose cooperation is needed for the team's suggestions to be accepted and implemented. And don't reward for projected savings before they are realized, unless you want to reward for effort rather than success. Finally, take care that the incentives you design for parallel team members don't create a conflict of interest between employees' regular job responsibilities and their part-time parallel team assignment. It's counterproductive, for example, to have employees cancelling important meetings they must attend to do their regular work because their parallel cost-reduction team has an incentive for having a meeting and coming up with new ideas. (Gross recommends giving team members recognition awards or merit bonuses for their regular jobs and for performance in the parallel team.)

As for the base pay component of parallel team members' compensation, skill-based pay can be a logical choice because it rewards team members for learning new problem-solving and analytical skills. But be sure to do a cost-benefit analysis here. It may be a waste of money to pay employees to learn skills for a parallel team that meets for only a few hours a week. If it is, Lawler and Cohen recommend, use job-based pay instead.

Compensating Project Teams

Parallel teams can often perform optimally without any changes to the existing compensation system. Adopting the team's suggestion may be its best reward. Project teams, however, require specially designed compensation plans because they often create something new. But the value of that new product or service may not be apparent until several years down the road, when data on market share and customer satisfaction becomes available.

Traditional compensation systems evaluate and reward performance on an annual basis, but compensation for project teams should be linked to the completion of the team's tasks. (It should also be adjusted if membership on the team changes over the course of the project.) Because it's hard to judge the effectiveness of a

Incentives for Teams

When crafting compensation systems for teams, keep in mind that:

Skill-Based Pay Alone May Not Get Teams Where You Want Them to Go

Literature dating back to experiments at Western Electric's Hawthorne plant in the 1920s and 1930s documents the productivity boosts that come from incentive pay.

Rewards Are Not the Most Important Element of a Performance-Management System

It's more important to define the team's objectives and establish mechanisms for reviewing and modifying behavior. These are the key drivers of team effectiveness. As USC's Cohen says, "Rewards should be a lag system rather than a lead system."

The Amount of Incentive Pay Must Be Meaningful

It takes incentive pay of at least a month's worth of salary—and a minimum of $1,000—to get a line

project team in the near term, it may make sense to reward group performance with gainsharing, or with a collective pay-for-performance system that covers not just the team but also the larger organizational unit. These options make good sense when the team's work has a major impact on the overall effectiveness of the unit, or when the time span of the team's project makes worker's attention. At Champion International, says Mark Childers, senior vice president for human resources, "It's not unusual for management teams to have incentive pay make up 40% of total compensation, with these bonuses dependent on the achievement of team goals."

Make Sure That Your Compensation System Gives First Priority to the Collective Goals

Within this framework, don't feel bad about naming and rewarding a "most valuable player," as long as the method of evaluation is clear.

Match the Incentive to the Value of the Task

If a successfully completed task has permanent value to the company, use a salary increase. If the task has only one-time value, reward it through a one-time bonus.

To Optimize the Team's Efforts, Express Incentives in Terms of Unit or Organizational Goals

This discourages teams from winning incentives at the expense of the overall unit or the company.

it difficult to measure and reward results because they won't be apparent until later.

It's tricky to manage, but experts believe that members of certain kinds of project teams should be rewarded for their individual contributions. Some biotechnology firms, for example, have devised a "walk on water" category for high performers (about 10% of employees).

Companies can assess the individuals' contributions at the end of a project by gathering peer and customer satisfaction ratings, and then melding these ratings with the organization's assessment of the success of the overall project. Managers usually like to exercise the prerogative of modifying peer and customer ratings on a case-by-case basis, but that can be counterproductive. Too many modifications may make the compensation appear subjective to employees.

Instead, consider canvassing the members of the team. They are often in the best position to evaluate each other's performance, even when the project team is heterogeneous. If the team members are mature, they will tend to be honest about rating each member's contribution, even if one member's work is valued at ten times the contribution of others on the team. In such situations, some companies award bonuses based on a set percentage of salary rather than the same fixed-dollar bonus for every member of the team. Champion International, the paper manufacturer based in Stamford, Conn., has created a formal bonus system that calculates project team bonuses using the midpoint of a salary grade. The employee's performance is rated on a scale of one through five. The lowest rating (none of the goals achieved) garners no bonus. The highest rating (all goals and then some met) yields a bonus of up to 34% of the salary range midpoint. At Champion, multipliers based on overall company performance can increase the size of the bonus even further.

Compensating Work Teams

Specially designed team incentives are often most effective for permanent, institutionalized work teams because their members are so interdependent. In the example of a manufacturing team in a highly automated oil refinery, one individual's work can affect everyone else's, and individual contributions are difficult to identify. A work team's objectives should be clearly defined, and the feedback systems and evaluation measures should be explicitly stated by the company.

Merit pay (in the form of salary increases or bonuses) and gainsharing plans can be effective ways to reward work teams. Companies may wish to distribute different rewards to different team members. Again, it's important to monitor the system you develop so that it doesn't undermine cooperation and group effort.

Lawler and Cohen believe that gainsharing is "particularly well suited to the participative nature of work teams. . . . It provides motivation for work teams to monitor their performance and learn about leverage points for improving performance." Starting in 1995, Champion International introduced an all-employee gainsharing award based on productivity. The results were so positive that the company expanded the program: half of all Champion's large factories now have gainsharing plans.

In some cases, however, gainsharing can be counterproductive, resulting in what Cohen refers to as "suboptimization at the group level." In one example, a geographically organized claims-processing team in an insurance company had incentives that effectively discouraged cooperation with work teams from other parts of the country, thereby impairing the company's overall performance. "In such instances," says Lawler, "the real issue is not whether to reward teams, but whether to reward individual teams or collections of teams." To prevent such suboptimization, Lawler recommends tying incentives to overall organizational goals so that various work teams will be motivated to collaborate.

The Team—and the Swamp

Crafting team-based performance metrics is complicated, fuzzy, highly nuanced work. If you are charged with doing it, the best advice is this: Override the urge to stick slavishly to guidelines, and focus instead on the particular needs of particular teams. Otherwise, instead of cheering "the team, the team, the team," you may be found wandering the halls of the organization muttering "the swamp, the swamp, the swamp." Your creativity will benefit your company and its teams. So might a pair of hip waders, and the exhortation "Go, team, go!"

For Further Reading

Compensation for Teams: How to Design and Implement Team-Based Rewards by Steven Gross (1995, AMACOM, 272 pp.)

Strategic Pay: Aligning Organizational Strategies and Pay Systems by Edward E. Lawler III (1990, Jossey-Bass, 328 pp.)

"Designing Pay Systems for Teams" by Edward E. Lawler III and Susan G. Cohen (*American Compensation Association Journal* Autumn 1992, pp. 6–18.)

"How the Right Measures Help Teams Excel" by C. Meyer (*Harvard Business Review,* May–June 1994, pp. 95–103.)

"Who Uses Skill-Based Pay, and Why" by Edward E. Lawler III, Gerald E. Ledford, Jr., and Lei Chang (*Compensation & Benefits Review,* 1993, pp. 22–26.)

Reprint U9711B

How to Reward
Project Teams

. . .

Project teams are everywhere these days, and companies depend on them more and more. If a team's work is added to members' regular jobs—or if it's unusually demanding for some other reason, such as a deadline requiring nights and weekends at the office—managers naturally want to find some way of rewarding participants.

But it isn't easy. Give them a bonus? A poorly conceived cash-award program can engender as much resentment as enthusiasm. Then again, noncash rewards—plaques, celebrations, gifts, and so forth—may ring hollow. "They motivate some people and not others," says Gerry Ledford, a principal with Sibson & Co.'s Los Angeles office.

To be sure, there's no perfect solution to the problem. But compensation experts offer tips for project-team compensation that can help you maximize the benefits and minimize potential damages.

Cash Payments

Make 'em Big

To be meaningful, a cash award has to be generous enough to get team members' attention. You may not want to go as far as Mike Armstrong, then-CEO of Hughes Electronics, who a few years ago divided up $20 million among 900 project engineers when they finished a Saudi Arabian air-defense system on schedule. But if you can't pay more than a token amount, choose the noncash route instead. A $50 check for (say) two months of hard work may be regarded more as an insult than as a reward.

Peg the Awards to Measurable Outcomes

Project-team bonuses are often pegged to milestones, says Steven E. Gross, a Philadelphia-based principal and director of employee pay practice for William M. Mercer. "The first milestone might be getting a design approved. A second could be planning the implementation. Third is getting some of the implementation done, and so forth. These are events that can be tracked and managed." Bringing in a project on time and on budget is another "milestone" that can be rewarded, adds Gross.

But Stay Focused on the Ultimate Goal

A milestone bonus must be vested when earned—but you may decide against paying it out right away. In a case reported in the book *Rewarding Teams: Lessons from the Trenches,* Lotus Development Corp. (Cambridge, Mass.) gave a team a bonus for making an April 27 interim deadline, but didn't pay it out until July 1. "We did it to make sure people didn't see April 27 as an end point," said team leader Larry Raymond. "There's a lot of emotional release upon hitting a major milestone, but we needed to keep pushing ahead."

Source of Funds? Get Creative

If a team's project involves a new product or revenue stream, Gross suggests rewarding members with a royalty arrangement or an award of additional stock. That way they're getting a "share of the potential gain for the future," rather than just a one-shot payout—and with a royalty arrangement they are rewarded only if their venture is successful. If the team's task involves cost saving, the award can be pegged to the costs that are saved, and it can be paid out as the savings are realized.

Let Members Divvy Up the Proceeds

While a manager at DuPont Co., Robert P. McNutt watched a team make difficult decisions about dividing up a bonus pool. "The team decided who was most deserving, who was the unofficial leader who made things happen," says McNutt, now a senior VP of HR at All First Financial in Baltimore. "That person might have gotten $3,000–$5,000, while maybe others got $500–$1,000. The team managed to come to an agreement, even though it meant that members "were deciding their own fate as well. They worked it through in an open, high-performance environment."

Watch for Undue Complexity—and Gaming

Cash awards are manageable when people in an organization participate in only one or two teams. But employees at some companies may serve on a dozen or more project groups. That can make an award system impossibly complex, since it has to take into account markedly different levels of participation among the members. It can also lead to political maneuvering. "You get people game playing—bagging the teams that look like they won't meet their goals and get an award, and fighting over who gets to be on the team that looks like it'll be successful," says Ledford.

Noncash Awards

"Noncash" Doesn't Always Mean "No Money"

At Utilicorp United, an energy company based in Kansas City, Mo., project teams that came up with cost-saving proposals were rewarded with monetary awards according to a predetermined schedule. But rather than writing an extra check to team members, the company gave them "UtiliBucks" to spend on merchandise chosen from a catalog. The rationale? Cash awards tend to go toward employees' everyday needs, while a directed-spending program like UtiliBucks forces them to buy something special. People "remember how they earned the video camera a lot longer than what they did with the same number of cash dollars," say the authors of *Rewarding Teams*.

Give Employees a Choice

Another advantage of a catalog-purchase program is that it lets employees choose their own rewards. That's a big issue in all kinds of noncash recognition plans, because it's so hard to create a one-size-fits-all program. "Any one award that you can come up with, some people will like and others won't," says Sibson's Ledford. Offering a choice doesn't require that you use a merchandise catalog of the UtiliBucks variety, only that you create a list of options. "Often companies will have a menu of ten choices—anything ranging from paying for maid service to movie tickets to dinner on the town."

Combine Cash and Noncash Awards

The drawback of a noncash award: if it's a token of recognition such as a plaque, it can be perceived as inadequate. But a cash award doesn't celebrate a team's accomplishments publicly. By all means pay a bonus or incentive, advises Robert McNutt, who is currently a faculty cadre leader on variable compensation at Worldat-Work (formerly American Compensation Association). But couple it with a public "thank you" to the team. "If your boss says what a heck of a job you did, you feel pretty good walking out the door on a Friday."

For Further Reading

Rewarding Teams: Lessons from the Trenches by Glenn Parker, Jerry McAdams, and David Zielinski (2000, Jossey-Bass)

Reprint U0007C

About the Contributors

Loren Gary is editor of Newsletters and Conferences Group at Harvard Business School Publishing.

Jim Billington is a contributor to *Harvard Management Update.*

Steve Barth was editor-at-large for the now-defunct *Knowledge Management* magazine. He lives in Long Beach, Calif.

Jim Biolos is a contributor to *Harvard Management Update.*

Jim Kling is a contributor to *Harvard Management Update.*

Mattison Crowe is a contributor to *Harvard Management Update.*

Rebecca M. Saunders is a freelance writer based in New York City.

David Stauffer is a Red Lodge, Mont.–based writer.

Charles Wardell is a contributor to *Harvard Management Update.*

Harvard Business Review Paperback Series

The Harvard Business Review Paperback Series offers the best thinking on cutting-edge management ideas from the world's leading thinkers, researchers, and managers. Designed for leaders who believe in the power of ideas to change business, these books will be useful to managers at all levels of experience, but especially senior executives and general managers. In addition, this series is widely used in training and executive development programs.

Books are priced at $19.95 U.S.
Price subject to change.

Title	Product #
Harvard Business Review **Interviews with CEOs**	3294
Harvard Business Review on **Advances in Strategy**	8032
Harvard Business Review on **Becoming a High Performance Manager**	1296
Harvard Business Review on **Brand Management**	1445
Harvard Business Review on **Breakthrough Leadership**	8059
Harvard Business Review on **Breakthrough Thinking**	181X
Harvard Business Review on **Building Personal and Organizational Resilience**	2721
Harvard Business Review on **Business and the Environment**	2336
Harvard Business Review on **Change**	8842
Harvard Business Review on **Compensation**	701X
Harvard Business Review on **Corporate Ethics**	273X
Harvard Business Review on **Corporate Governance**	2379
Harvard Business Review on **Corporate Responsibility**	2748
Harvard Business Review on **Corporate Strategy**	1429
Harvard Business Review on **Crisis Management**	2352
Harvard Business Review on **Culture and Change**	8369
Harvard Business Review on **Customer Relationship Management**	6994
Harvard Business Review on **Decision Making**	5572
Harvard Business Review on **Effective Communication**	1437

Title	Product #
Harvard Business Review on **Entrepreneurship**	9105
Harvard Business Review on **Finding and Keeping the Best People**	5564
Harvard Business Review on **Innovation**	6145
Harvard Business Review on **Knowledge Management**	8818
Harvard Business Review on **Leadership**	8834
Harvard Business Review on **Leadership at the Top**	2756
Harvard Business Review on **Leading in Turbulent Times**	1806
Harvard Business Review on **Managing Diversity**	7001
Harvard Business Review on **Managing High-Tech Industries**	1828
Harvard Business Review on **Managing People**	9075
Harvard Business Review on **Managing the Value Chain**	2344
Harvard Business Review on **Managing Uncertainty**	9083
Harvard Business Review on **Managing Your Career**	1318
Harvard Business Review on **Marketing**	8040
Harvard Business Review on **Measuring Corporate Performance**	8826
Harvard Business Review on **Mergers and Acquisitions**	5556
Harvard Business Review on **Motivating People**	1326
Harvard Business Review on **Negotiation**	2360
Harvard Business Review on **Nonprofits**	9091
Harvard Business Review on **Organizational Learning**	6153
Harvard Business Review on **Strategic Alliances**	1334
Harvard Business Review on **Strategies for Growth**	8850
Harvard Business Review on **The Business Value of IT**	9121
Harvard Business Review on **The Innovative Enterprise**	130X
Harvard Business Review on **Turnarounds**	6366
Harvard Business Review on **What Makes a Leader**	6374
Harvard Business Review on **Work and Life Balance**	3286

Management Dilemmas:
Case Studies from the Pages of
Harvard Business Review

How often do you wish you could turn to a panel of experts to guide you through tough management situations? The Management Dilemmas series provides just that. Drawn from the pages of *Harvard Business Review,* each insightful volume poses several perplexing predicaments and shares the problem-solving wisdom of leading experts. Engagingly written, these solutions-oriented collections help managers make sound judgment calls when addressing everyday management dilemmas.

These books are priced at $19.95 U.S.
Price subject to change.

To order, call 1-800-668-6780, or go online at www.HBSPress.org

Harvard Business Essentials

In the fast-paced world of business today, everyone needs a personal resource—a place to go for advice, coaching, background information, or answers. The Harvard Business Essentials series fits the bill. Concise and straightforward, these books provide highly practical advice for readers at all levels of experience. Whether you are a new manager interested in expanding your skills or an experienced executive looking to stay on top, these solution-oriented books give you the reliable tips and tools you need to improve your performance and get the job done. Harvard Business Essentials titles will quickly become your constant companions and trusted guides.

These books are priced at $19.95 U.S., except as noted.
Price subject to change.

The Results-Driven Manager

The Results-Driven Manager series collects timely articles from *Harvard Management Update* and *Harvard Management Communication Letter* to help senior to middle managers sharpen their skills, increase their effectiveness, and gain a competitive edge. Presented in a concise, accessible format to save managers valuable time, these books offer authoritative insights and techniques for improving job performance and achieving immediate results.

These books are priced at $14.95 U.S.
Price subject to change.

Title	Product #
The Results-Driven Manager: **Face-to-Face Communications for Clarity and Impact**	3477
The Results-Driven Manager: **Managing Yourself for the Career You Want**	3469
The Results-Driven Manager: **Presentations That Persuade and Motivate**	3493
The Results-Driven Manager: **Teams That Click**	3507
The Results-Driven Manager: **Winning Negotiations That Preserve Relationships**	3485

Readers of the Results-Driven Manager series find the following Harvard Business School Press books of interest.

If you find these books useful:	You may also like these:
Presentations That Persuade and Motivate	Working the Room (8199)
Face-to-Face Communications for Clarity and Impact	HBR on Effective Communication (1437)
	HBR on Managing People (9075)
Winning Negotiations That Preserve Relationships	HBR on Negotiation (2360)
	HBE Guide to Negotiation (1113)
Teams That Click	The Wisdom of Teams (3670)
	Leading Teams (3332)
Managing Yourself for the Career You Want	Primal Leadership (486X)
	Leading Quietly (4878)
	Leadership on the Line (4371)

How to Order

Harvard Business School Press publications are available worldwide
from your local bookseller or online retailer.
You can also call

1-800-668-6780

Our product consultants are available to help you
8:00 a.m.–6:00 p.m., Monday–Friday, Eastern Time.
Outside the U.S. and Canada, call: 617-783-7450
Please call about special discounts for quantities greater than ten.

You can order online at

www.HBSPress.org